# Absent Memories

*Moving forward when you can't look back*

Strength does not come from winning.
Your struggles develop your strengths.
When you go through hardships and
decide not to surrender, that is strength.
—*Arnold Schwarzenegger*

Rebecah Propst

*Absent Memories: Moving Forward When You Can't Look Back*

Published by Wheatmark, 610 East Delano Street, Suite 104,
Tucson, Arizona 85705 U.S.A., www.wheatmark.com

*Cover photography provided by Photos.com*
*Author photograph by Carol LaBelle-Propst*

Publisher's Cataloging-In-Publication Data
(Prepared by The Donohue Group, Inc.)

Propst, Rebecah.
  Absent memories : moving forward when you can't look back / by
Rebecah Propst.

   p. ; cm.

  ISBN: 978-1-58736-842-4

1. Propst, Rebecah. 2. Amnesiacs—Biography. 3. Epileptics—
Biography.

I. Title.

RC394.A5 P76 2007
362.196/85232/092     2007925281

*To Jim*
*With all my love*

*Absent Memories: Moving Forward When You Can't Look Back* is the true story of my life to the best of my ability to recall it. Names of people and places have been changed to preserve privacy.

> All photographs are accurate. None of
> them is the truth.
>
> —*Richard Avedon*

My sister was pointing at pictures in the old family photo album.

"Here's Peter. You never went anywhere without that little stuffed elephant. Remember?"

"Here you are as the Statue of Liberty on the float Dad made when he ran for the state legislature. Remember?"

"I don't know what you were working on here. You were always building something in the shop on the ranch. Remember?"

"Here's that red convertible. Dad was so proud of it. We hated it; we had to bend over to keep our hair from getting messed up. Remember?"

"Take a look at these hairstyles! We really thought we looked gorgeous. Remember?"

"Here you are working on Dad's prototype timber harvester. Everyone called you Rosie the Riveter then. Remember?"

"You managed that quick printing franchise for two years. Remember?"

"Here you are running the Marine Corps Marathon in Washington DC. Remember?"

"Here we all are at your final test for your black belt. Remember?"

"That's an article you wrote when you got back from your trip to Bolivia when you were in the National Guard. Remember?"

I tried to act interested, but I didn't remember any of them. They were images of the life of a stranger.

# Preface

"**F**orget the past."
"Live in the present."
"All we have is this moment in time."

The sages who spout these snippets of conventional
wisdom are clueless. They have no concept of how
important every single past experience is to a meaningful
present.

Nine years ago, just before my forty-seventh birthday,
I was starting to get reacquainted with myself. On Halloween, 1997, I had my last grand mal seizure. I don't remember
anything of my life prior to that time, and memories of the
following few months are fuzzy and selective. Most people
with seizures experience some memory loss, but rarely is it
as comprehensive as mine is. It wasn't like forgetting where
I put my keys; I no longer had any experiences, friends, or
identity. I no longer had a past.

I was an adult, but the world was new to me. I'd have
to rebuild my life on the slippery foundation of the present.
My success would depend on my insatiable curiosity, my
intense survival instinct, my good health, and the ability I
still had to read, write, and learn.

At first, I didn't see a problem. Life was a fascinating

enigma, but I felt that there was undoubtedly a logical explanation for everything. If I kept my eyes open, I could decipher it. Granted, there was a lot to learn, but how hard could that be? I was a novice anticipating the thrill of a whitewater ride. The turbulence would be a challenge, but others seemed to feel at home on the rivers of their lives—all I had to do was discover what they knew. It might be tricky at first, and it would take a little time, but as soon as I understood how everything worked, I could choose a river—any river—and enjoy the ride.

Now, nine years later, I've learned how impossible that vision was. My expedition has been, for the most part, terrifying. I've spent most of my time frantically flailing as I tumbled through life's impetuous waters. Periodically, when my river flattened, I shook the water from my eyes and tried to comprehend what happened. I've experienced the exhilaration of pure discovery, the satisfaction of developing practical skills, and the acute frustration of ignorance. I've learned how to breathe between somersaults through the rocks, but I have a long way to go before I understand much of my river—a river I did not choose, a river that would have been impossible to ride without the new memories I collected along the way.

# One

My life as I remember it began around that auspicious
Halloween, a few months before my forty-eighth
birthday. I was living in Tumbleweed, a small town on the
eastern Colorado plains. I lived alone in an ancient, rickety,
three-room, second-story, *dinky* apartment.

My earliest memories of the place were that it felt and
smelled gray. It was debatable whether the previous renters
owned any cleaning supplies, and the landlord apparently
wasn't interested in maintenance. I hated it, so I checked
other rentals in town. None of them had a bedroom large
enough for my king-sized waterbed. I was stuck there. I'd
have to do whatever I could to make it livable.

The partial wall between the kitchen and living room
made the apartment feel an inch or two bigger than it was.
A huge plant dominated the room, no matter where I put
him. (I later learned that he was a tree philodendron I had
named Beauregard over twenty years ago.) I was forever
squeezing my love seat, stereo, TV, and wicker end tables
into innovative arrangements to make the living room feel
more spacious. If I pushed my old, round, glass-topped,

wobbly, wicker dining table up against the kitchen wall, there was just enough room to walk around it. The bed and a bookcase full of interesting-looking books barely fit into the tiny bedroom. From the bedroom, I could see my old white Volkswagen Jetta parked on the street under a big shade tree.

The old, wood-framed windows provided a lot of light, but they were tricky to operate. It took a lot of prying, grunting, and cussing to get one of the living room windows to open at all. The other one opened easily but wouldn't stay open without some kind of prop. The small kitchen window simply refused to budge. The bedroom window worked fine, but its screen seemed to be hanging on by whatever screens use for fingernails. If I was lucky, an occasional summer cross-breeze found its way between those temperamental spaces.

I decided to see if a good cleaning would make the place tolerable, so I read instructions on bottles of cleaning products and experimented with various scrubbing sponges, brushes, and balls of curly metal. I spent my spare time washing walls and doors, scrubbing sinks, shining windows, and chipping hard water deposits off the bathroom fixtures. I moved the stove and refrigerator to scour and wax every inch of the kitchen floor. I found an old rug to cover a hole in the disintegrating, but at least clean, linoleum in front of the bathroom "vanity." When I was finally finished, the apartment seemed bigger, smelled better, and felt lighter.

I had solved one of my life's problems, my grungy apartment, by learning. I believed any problem could be solved the same way: by investigating all the possible solutions, learning how to do whatever was necessary, and then just doing it.

# Two

The ability to express an idea is well nigh
as important as the idea itself.
              —*Bernard M. Baruch*

I knew I had a lot to learn. However, I didn't think learning to communicate was anywhere on the list. I knew hundreds of beautiful words, each with their own nuances. I used every grammatically correct word combination I could come up with to explain my situation. I scoured my dictionary for even more precise words. Each attempt was more brilliant than the last. Each attempt failed miserably. Everyone seemed bewildered. After a pause, they all asked the same questions.

The most common question was, "What did you forget?" At first, I wanted to grab questioners by the neck and demand, "What part of 'everything' don't you understand?" Frustrated, I couldn't even imagine what kinds of things they thought I should be able to remember!

After doing some research, I learned that, medically speaking, I'd lost my long-term declarative memory, but my implicit memory seemed to be relatively intact. (See appendix.) For example, I couldn't remember my childhood on the farm, but I believed in hard work and responsibility. I didn't remember what I'd learned on past jobs, but I knew I had to make money to pay for rent, food, and gasoline. I didn't know what a good diet was, but I knew I had to take care of my body. I couldn't remember the official rules of the road, but I knew how to drive. My closet was full of unfamiliar stuff—skis, a camera, roller blades, a revolver, a bow and arrows, a tennis racket, and a black-belted karate uniform. I didn't know how to use these things, but I knew I had to stretch before I went for a run. I couldn't remember my mother, who died more than ten years ago, but I knew my father, stepmother, and two sisters were all members of the same family. I didn't know the person I'd been throughout my life, but various people told me I seemed to have the same personality and mannerisms I'd always had. In other words, I didn't remember any facts, details, experiences, or people from my past. A computer geek might have said that I'd lost some data from my hard drive, but my operating system was apparently unaffected.

One thing that was puzzling was my retention of some memories that I now consider to be, strictly speaking, declarative. For example, I knew the words and melodies of dozens of songs. I also understood the meanings of hundreds of words. It's still hard to explain those apparent exceptions to the declarative/implicit rule. The only explanation I've come up with is that the brain is so complex and its processes so intricate that anything is possible.

Most people also wanted to know what happened. That's still a difficult question to answer, even for the experts. My neurologist told me that seizures caused my memory loss, but he couldn't tell me exactly how that happened. The notations in my medical records weren't particularly helpful, either. Apparently, none of the doctors I'd consulted could find a physical reason for either my memory loss or my seizures. All anyone seemed to know was I started having seizures in my early forties, once a month, right after my period.

Doctors at the Mayo Clinic told me I had epilepsy,

a disorder that causes a variety of repeated seizures. They diagnosed mine as "complex partial temporal lobe seizures with an unknown cause." (See appendix.) Partial seizures can worsen and become grand mal seizures, the full-body convulsions most people are familiar with. That's exactly what happened to me. Even today, doctors can't pinpoint a cause for most kinds of epilepsy. All they can do is try to find something to stop the seizures. What works for one person might not work for anyone else. Many people never find a medication or a combination of medications that will completely control their seizures.

Apparently, the traditional anticonvulsants hadn't worked for me. From the huge stack of receipts I later found, it looked like I'd consulted traditional doctors and every kind of homeopath imaginable searching for my own seizure stopper. The exhaustive search took more than seven years. It finally ended in Tumbleweed when I was referred to the neurologist who found my personal miracle drug; Lamictal had been released in February of 1997, eight months prior to my last seizure.

One of my very first memories was the day I met Hank. Sometime after I picked up my first prescription, I had gone to the local McDonald's. The eighty-one-year-old man I saw there seemed vaguely familiar. I asked if I could sit with him. As we sipped our coffee, he told me we'd already met. I didn't remember that meeting or anything else about him. When I told him I had epilepsy, he told me he lived less than a block from me. He wrote down his address and phone number, and told me to call or go to his house if I ever needed help.

My memories of that time period are so sketchy that they are almost nonexistent. I do, however, remember one in particular. I woke up in the middle of the night. I was standing beside my bed. My head hurt. I didn't know what had happened, but I was scared. *Had I had a seizure?* While

I was trying to decide what to do, I remembered what Hank had said. I dressed quickly and ran to his house.

"Call your doctor," Hank said immediately.

"It's the middle of the night," I whimpered. "I don't even know if I had a seizure or not."

"Maybe if you explain how you feel, he'll be able to tell," Hank suggested.

I couldn't decide. *What if it was nothing?* I paced back and forth, arguing with myself.

"He wouldn't have given you his home phone number if he didn't want you to use it," Hank said, handing me the phone.

I dialed the number nervously and told the doctor what had happened.

"It sounds like you did have a seizure, Beki," he said. "Let's increase your dosage and see if that works."

That was my last grand mal seizure.

That neurologist believed my epilepsy was hormonally related. He wasn't sure exactly how or when my seizures did their dirty work, but he believed they eliminated my store of long-term memories as certainly as the delete key erases data from a hard drive.

The doctor explained that our brains are, in fact, a lot like computers. They assimilate experiences and information and store everything in our memory for later access. I don't think my memories were erased all at once. The term that best describes a seizure for me is "brain storm." It makes sense that a seizure's intense electrical commotion might damage some memory cells or neurotransmitters. In my case, by the time I had my last convulsion that Halloween, it's possible that whatever stored my long-term memories was finally wiped clean.

My doctor's explanation made sense. However, "psychosomatic memory loss" was always a specter in the background. I was told that I'd been laid off, my mother had died, my husband had left, and I'd had a radical mastectomy to treat breast cancer—all around the time I was having seizures. The possibility that I had forgotten my life just because it was hard to handle suggested I might not be emotionally strong enough to deal with it in the future. That was a weakness I couldn't afford.

For several months after my last full-body convulsion, I still had problems with my short-term memory. I believe I was probably still having partial seizures. I'm not sure when the medicine finally controlled all my seizures, but when it did, my newly quiet brain was again able to store a continuous stream of data, information I could retrieve and use.

Inevitably, in every conversation, after a pause, people usually said—and still do say—something like, "I'm sorry. That must be awful for you." I'm not sure why they think that. No one thinks it's awful that they don't remember the first few years of their own lives.

If you have no memory of an experience, it's as if it never happened. We constantly observe, do, think, study, move, relate. We process our experiences logically. We react to them emotionally. We use them to deepen our understanding of ourselves and our universe. We store them in our brains. After we experience a loss, we relive our memories and understand that what we lost will no longer be available to us. *That* understanding is what's awful.

In my case, my family lives all over the country. All my remembered life, I've lived by myself. How can I miss living in a family?

I have a diploma that shows I have a bachelor's degree, but the only college class I can remember is one I took after my last seizure. The first dorm room I remember seeing was my nephew's, when I visited him at his college. How can I miss my own college experience?

I found passports stamped for Bolivia and Tahiti in a trunk. Someone told me I'd gone to Bolivia when I was a member of the Colorado National Guard. I found out what the National Guard was, but I couldn't imagine what motivated me to enlist. My trip to Tahiti was apparently part of a college anthropology field trip. I found the tiny island on a globe and tried to imagine what it was like and why it would be interesting to an anthropologist. How can I miss experiences that, as far as I know, I didn't have?

I don't remember my husbands. The last one left after I started having seizures. Pictures of him are images of a stranger. My family says I believed he was my soul mate, but I don't remember anything of our life together. If you have no memory of a person, it's as if you never met. How can I grieve for someone I don't know?

I'm told I held some impressive, high-paying jobs. My only memories, however, are of low-paying, mindless jobs. How can I miss the advantages of a good salary and challenging work?

In other words, how can it be awful to lose what you've never had?

Another common reaction is an emotional pat on the back: "I'm sure your memories will come back to you," people say. From the beginning, however, I've known I can't grope for memories and trust that they'll eventually surface. My memories are permanently, irretrievably lost. None of the details of my prior life will ever exist for me.

Others take an upbeat approach. "Well, that's not all bad," they chuckle. "There are a lot of things I'd like to forget." Or, "If you think about it, that's exciting. You get to start over!" The possibility of a new beginning may sound enticing, but I didn't get to choose which memories to leave behind. I'd lost all my friends as well as enemies. I'd lost all my experiences—good as well as bad. I'd lost the information and skills I'd gained through those experiences. I couldn't reshape my future by avoiding past errors. I had to build a new life from scratch.

It was frustrating. How could something so simple be so hard to explain?

# Three

Dealing with the loss of the past, itself, wasn't difficult. My past simply didn't exist. I didn't know enough about what I'd had in that past to feel anything about what was missing from my life now. I didn't know enough about the world to compare my current situation with that of anyone else. I had no idea what I was missing, so I couldn't feel sad or angry or disappointed or jealous or upset. I saw the world as a baby must see it. Everything was new or yet to be discovered.

Dealing with the consequences of my loss was a different matter. Unlike a baby, I had no one to introduce me to the world. It took a while for me to understand that many of the things I "just knew" to be true were mere assumptions. For example, I just knew that once people understood my situation, they'd adapt to it effortlessly. New acquaintances would instantly understand that our friendship could be built only on future shared experiences. My family and friends would understand that we'd have to get reacquainted and establish new and different relationships. Employers would easily agree to give me more training than other employees. This viewpoint certainly felt right.

However, it was based on the mistaken belief that people could truly understand my situation at all.

For me, my past was irrelevant. It couldn't be anything else. Discovering the person I'd been before I lost my memory might be interesting, but what did it matter? What did that person's childhood home, friends, or hobbies have to do with me?

No one seemed to agree with me. Everyone maintained that it was essential to rediscover what I'd forgotten. My father was one of the most insistent. He told me, "You need to know where you came from, who you are." I couldn't understand it. I knew who I was. I was the person standing right in front of him.

Finally, I agreed to investigate, primarily to shut everybody up. I visited my childhood home, called people from my past, met relatives, looked at myriads of pictures, and listened to dozens of stories. I learned where I'd lived, what schools I'd attended, where I'd worked, what men I'd married, *blah, blah, blah.* The resulting history was fragmented, distorted, and contradictory. After a while, I assembled a bunch of details about my past life and accomplishments—a collection of biographical information about someone I didn't know. None of those facts resonated with me, but they seemed to be critical to everyone else.

Another of the things I unconsciously believed was that friendships were natural consequences of living. Mine would be fundamentally the same as any other; my missing past would barely be noticeable. I looked forward to making friends and learning about the world through their eyes. All I had to do was meet people and friendships would develop.

There was just one minor problem. I didn't really know how to meet people. I knew there had to be some kind of accepted procedure involved in getting acquainted, so I set out to learn it. My dad had been involved in politics for much of his life. He'd explained how he'd made a living working with people to solve problems. Everyone seemed to like him. If anyone would know how to get acquainted, he would.

"Look people in the eye, shake their hands, and smile," he advised. "And don't give them a weak, girly handshake," he said, taking my hand and gripping it firmly.

"Don't be afraid to ask questions," Dad added. "People love to talk about themselves and share what they know. Most people will be honored that you asked. In fact, they'll probably think you're the most interesting person they've met, even if you don't say a word."

His advice turned out to be pivotal. I started to meet all kinds of people, and my learning curve skyrocketed with each acquaintance.

Over time, however, I started to understand that memories play a much larger role in friendships than I'd imagined. References to the past crop up in almost every discussion. "Man, these CDs are a far cry from the old records, aren't they?" *What are records?* "If you've got the bucks, you never go to jail. Look at O.J. Simpson." *What does money have to do with staying out of jail? Who's O.J. Simpson?* "Watergate was Nixon's downfall." *What was Watergate? Who was Nixon?* "I spent many a night draggin' Main in that old Studebaker." *What's "draggin' Main"? What's a Studebaker?* "My first girlfriend was a hippie." *What's a hippie?* "Come in! You don't have to knock; you're my sister." *What's so special about being a sister?* Everyone's reminiscences were fun, and my imagination always got a workout, but my ignorance of "the good old days" quickly became more frustrating than my ignorance of my own history. My questions were hiccups that interrupted each conversation.

I'm not a victim of an illness where memory loss is just one of many recognizable symptoms. It isn't apparent. As my knowledge base broadens, I can carry on casual conversations and intelligent discussions without mentioning it. Even today, however, I'm often asked how I felt about something that happened in my past. Sometimes, I try a nonanswer, like "The way anyone would feel, I guess." Or I try to deflect the question with one of my own: "How would you feel?" Sometimes, I can steer the conversation back to the other person and prolong it. Eventually, however, if we talk long enough, there's no way around the questions, and I have to admit that I don't know how I felt, and explain why. Whenever that happens, the focus of the conversation shifts, along with the nature of the relationship. No matter how much I learn, I'll never be able to share my childhood on the farm, my ski trips, or my experiences as a wife. There will always be gaps in each of my relationships where we can never connect.

Interacting with people I knew in the past is much more difficult than establishing new relationships. Part of the reason could be that the few people who stayed in contact with me didn't live nearby. Members of my immediate family were scattered all over the country. My father lived on the East Coast; one sister lived on the West Coast and the other two hours away. My college roommate also lived two hours away.

For years, my family and friends seemed slightly perplexed whenever I told them I didn't remember something we'd done together or who we'd been to each other. They answered my specific questions but didn't offer additional information about things they must have believed I already knew. As a result, my perceptions of those past relationships were disjointed and conflicting.

I had put as much faith in others' ability to explain the world as in my own ability to explain what had happened to me. Over time, I started to see that words, the only tools I had then, weren't enough. It didn't matter how precise they were. It didn't matter how I put them together in a sentence. If they didn't express memories, it was hard for people to relate to what I was saying. I started to wonder if memories somehow made us "real" to each other.

Alone in my miniature living room one summer day, I realized that just as no one would be able to fully comprehend my loss, I'd never be able to understand what it was like to live a "normal" life. I started to appreciate how different my associations would always be from those of everyone else. Friendships were apparently more complex than I had imagined. They seemed to be ethereal, even fragile. They seemed to require some kind of emotional interaction and commitment I couldn't fathom. I realized it might not be possible for me to develop any true friendships at all.

*Does it really matter, anyway?* I wondered. From what I could tell, friendships made you feel good, but they didn't seem necessary for survival. Since survival would have to be my top priority for quite a while, friendships were a luxury I might not ever have time to experience.

*Do I like myself enough to be able to live without friends completely?* I asked myself. I thought a minute. I liked my sense of humor. I had a stereo and piles of records, tapes, and CDs. I had a library card. I had some running shoes. I'd already spent a lot of time alone, having fun all by myself.

I decided I liked myself well enough. I'd just have to make sure I'd always be the kind of person I enjoyed being with.

# Four

Ignorance is defined as "the condition of being uneducated, unaware, or uninformed" (*American Heritage Dictionary*). I couldn't remember any of my formal education. I was unaware of my past experiences or what a normal life was like. I was uninformed about how things worked, why people acted the way they did, or what consequences my choices would have. I was ignorant.

That ignorance didn't concern me at first. A German proverb, "Nothing is as new as something which has long been forgotten," describes how I felt. I was like a kitten; I didn't know what to look at or listen to or try to understand. My world was an awesome place. Nature was magical and endlessly fascinating. I didn't think anything could be more fun than learning about it. Life was a gigantic puzzle I couldn't wait to solve. I looked forward to a thrilling adventure of discovery, fueled by inquisitiveness and limited only by the amount of work I chose to do.

I watched and wondered. Tumbleweed was a small, old town, and it was full of nature. The colorful flowers planted alongside the tidy houses always seemed to be smiling. On my walk home, the breathtaking sight of sparkling green leaves set against a sunny, Colorado sky full of puffballs sparked dozens of questions. *Why are leaves green? What make them glisten? Why is the sky blue? What are clouds made of? What causes rainbows?* I sat on the lawn for hours one night, watching a harvest moon move slowly through a cloudless sky. I stopped in the middle of a run one day to study the seemingly well-coordinated activity of a hill of red ants. When robins hopped across our front lawn, heads cocked, I wondered if they could really hear worms moving underground. *Speaking of worms, why did they crawl into the street when it rained? How about centipedes? How did they walk without tripping themselves up?*

Life's mysteries weren't all found outside. I wanted to know everything there was to know about the human body. *Why was it harder to climb stairs than to walk down a hill? What made some people nearsighted? What made our hearts beat automatically? How did broken bones heal? Why had I developed epilepsy? How had my memories been erased?*

People's activities were almost as fascinating as Mother Nature's. My dad had been a history teacher early in his career. His tales of humanity's adventures through time were more interesting than fiction—they were certainly more implausible. The devices people had invented were fascinating, too. Some were practical, like tools or farm equipment. Others were just plain fun, like merry-go-rounds or kaleidoscopes. I wanted to know all about them. *How could a moving steering wheel change the way tires point? How did a welding iron work? Why were there flaps on airplane wings? How did you steer a kite? What made bubbles fluorescent? How did glass crystals make rainbows on the wall? How was glass made, anyway?*

I looked everywhere for answers to my unlimited questions. I took my dad's advice and learned how to use the local library's computer. At my sister's suggestion, I took a cell biology class at the local junior college where I learned about the building blocks of life, down to the last electron. I read tons of books. My *American Heritage Dictionary* gave me the meanings of words; sometimes it even had pictures of those pocket-sized descriptions of pieces of the world! When the signal was strong enough for my old antenna, I watched documentaries on TV. I used my imagination to swim through the amazing human body, zoom through the limitless numbers of stars, and absorb the magic created by light and sound waves.

Some of the things I learned were more practical than fun. I knew I had to eat a balanced diet, but I didn't know how to cook. I bought TV dinners for lunch and supper. I'd heard that vegetables were important, so I alternated cereal with peas for breakfast. Cooking seemed like a waste of time. Why would anyone want to spend a lot of time on something that disappeared in a few minutes? (It took almost two years for one of my friends to talk me into letting him teach me how to fry an egg.)

Math is another example. To relearn how to balance my checkbook, I read the instructions on my bank statements over and over. I got my neighbor to show me how to use a calculator. I worked on adding, subtracting, and multiplying in my head during my daily runs. I subtracted the number of minutes I'd run from the minutes of my total run, sometimes counting on my fingers. I tried to figure out how much of the run I'd completed by dividing the total minutes by the completed minutes. *Wait, could that be right? What if I divided the completed minutes by the total minutes?* I had to refigure the final total over and over to come up with the same number more than once, and then decide if it was a number that made sense.

Experience was my greatest teacher. Sometimes I initiated an experience to see what would happen. Like the time I decided to turn the weedy strip alongside our apartment building into a garden. My neighbor showed me how to plant and care for the vegetables and flowers that would grow there, and I watched Mother Nature at work.

Many times, however, the things I learned just happened. One day I got my bike out of my closet and decided to take it for a spin. I had to relearn how to ride it. I figured out how the brakes worked and took off. After I could ride without losing my balance, I watched what happened when I switched gears. (I assumed the round plate thingies were gears.) *What did the size of the gears have to do with speed?*

I never really thought about the tires until the bike started to seem sluggish one day. At first, I assumed my bike-riding muscles had just weakened. The farther I went, however, the harder it got. I kept looking at the tires, and finally decided they were getting flat. I couldn't understand it; they'd been fine on my last bike ride. I got off and walked home.

When I got there, my neighbor was smoking on the front step. A short, skinny guy with a grumpy manner and a rare smile, Vern took one look at the now-frayed tires and loaded the bike into his van. On the way to the bike shop, he explained slow leaks. When we got back, he showed me how to use my bicycle pump (which until then had been just another mysterious object in my closet.) So much for "It's just like riding a bike."

Shortly after that, I learned that ignorance could be more than just an innocent lack of information. One day, when I opened the door to my apartment, an unusual, disgusting odor hit me. I assumed it was just another of the little rat trap's eccentricities, but it got worse as I walked into the kitchen.

As usual, my neighbor's door was open, and I hadn't closed mine yet. "Hey, Vern," I yelled. "What's that smell?"

He sauntered over. "That's gas, honey. Your pilot light must be out."

I had no idea what he meant by "pilot light." He took

me into the kitchen and showed me where the little flame should be. I quickly found some matches and pulled one out of the box. It'd probably take all the matches I had to get rid of that gross smell.

"Wait a minute!" He grabbed the match before I could strike it. "If you light this, you could blow the whole place up!"

"Yeah, right," I said, assuming he was making one of his usual jokes.

Vern snatched the matchbox and looked behind the stove. He closed a valve, told me to open all the windows, then pointed me to the door. We went downstairs and sat on the front step. He lit a cigarette and told me about natural gas. The more he explained, the more the glowing tip of his cigarette brought to mind visions of a fiery explosion. I breathed a sigh of relief when he put it out in the rusty old can beside the step and led me back upstairs. The smell was barely noticeable. Vern watched while I reopened the valve and nervously lit the small flame.

It was scary to learn that ignorance could be physically dangerous. I was about to discover how it could affect a career.

# Five

Life is not a spectacle or a feast. It is a predicament.

—*George Santayana*

I was selling advertising for a country music radio station. It was the first job I can remember. I don't know how I got it. The base pay didn't cover my living expenses; I was banking on future commissions. I firmly believed that by working hard, I could make more than enough money to pay the bills.

The station owner, Mr. Heinrich, was a tall man with an expressionless face, dominating demeanor, and German accent. He rarely smiled when he greeted me each morning. One day, he added a stern reprimand to his greeting.

"When I say 'Good morning,' I expect you to do the same!"

Startled, I told him I always had.

"Well, I can't hear you," he said grimly.

"Good morning," I said, more loudly than usual. He nodded curtly and went into his office. *What was that all about?* He was obviously annoyed, and I was upset. *Was I breaking some kind of unwritten behavior code?*

I couldn't take time to think about that then. I'd set a goal to personally call on all the businesses in town. I hurried outside and jumped into my Jetta.

My short-term memory was still extremely tenuous.

After each sales call, I raced to my car and picked up my Day-Timer. I drew a small map of the inside of the business, a physical description of the people I'd spoken to, where I'd found them in the building, and what we'd discussed. If I could remember anything else by then, I'd scribble that, too. I copied information from their business card and repeated it aloud, hoping to drill it into my brain. Sometimes that worked.

After three months, I was eligible for health insurance benefits. When I asked about them, the office manager assured me she'd sent in the paperwork. "You know how insurance companies are," she sighed, shaking her head. I wondered what she meant. I didn't remember anything about insurance companies.

Fortunately, as time passed, my short-term memory improved. I didn't need as many notes. I could concentrate more on how to satisfy each customer's needs. It took longer than I expected, but my salesmanship improved, and I made a few small sales. One day, I sold one of the largest advertising packages the station offered. I believed, with that customer as a reference, future sales would be easier.

That theory would never be tested. After she signed the contract, my customer was approached by the other radio station in town. They offered a better package at a third of the cost. She was furious, and I immediately empathized with her. *So that's why it had been so hard for me to build a client base!* Mr. Heinrich had insisted from the start that the prices were nonnegotiable. How could I sell anything if I couldn't compete?

My supervisor, Percy, was the sales manager. I drove back to the station and stormed into his office. After he heard what had happened, he just sat there. I tried to reason with him. He obviously didn't share my concern. I kept talking. I demanded that he do something to make things right with her. He finally agreed to go see her. When we got to my customer's shop, Percy stood in the middle of the floor. He didn't look at her while she spoke. He seemed to be completely indifferent. Finally, without expressing a shred of regret, he walked out and drove off.

I decided to take my case to Mr. Heinrich. For days, I carefully prepared my arguments. While I was at it, I added several other suggestions to improve our overall customer service.

He listened impassively before commenting, "It seems you're not happy here."

I was confused. *Why was he changing the subject? I* thought about his question. I hated commercials, and I hated country music. His arrogance was irritating, and the sales manager's apathy was exasperating. But I liked meeting everyone in town and learning about their businesses.

*Wait a minute! What did my feelings have to do with anything, anyway? I was doing my job. I was making money for him. I was just making a few recommendations.* I didn't know how to answer.

He must have taken my silence for agreement.

"Linda will send you your final check. Good luck."

I was staggered. This just didn't make sense. My instincts had told me that if I was honest, worked hard, and treated people the way I liked to be treated, I would eventually succeed. Apparently, I was mistaken. As I walked to my car, I tried to understand what I'd done wrong. *Had I been out of line by defending my customer's complaint? Was I wrong to make suggestions? Were my sales too low? Was my tone of voice or body language offensive?* Maybe taking care of the customer wasn't the way to succeed. After all, Heinrich had owned the radio station for over twenty years.

Later, I was told that his salesmen never lasted long enough to collect health insurance benefits. Right then, however, the possibility that Heinrich's decision might have nothing to do with me didn't cross my mind. I was sure my ignorance had cost me my job.

It took five minutes to drive home, climb the stairs, and open my apartment door. For the first time, I realized I'd lost more than a bunch of insignificant details. I didn't know what I'd lost, where to look for it, or even how to recognize it if I ran into it. I took a good, hard look at my life. I might have twenty-five or thirty years left. I obviously knew nothing about the world of work. I didn't know what jobs were out there, what I needed to know or do to get one of those jobs, what would be expected of me after I was hired, or how to behave around coworkers and supervisors.

My top priority, learning how to support myself, had instantly become a colossal boulder in my river. I wanted to scream or cry or punch something, but I couldn't afford to waste time on negative emotions. I had to keep a clear head and figure out what to do, immediately. In spite of that resolve, an unfamiliar feeling saturated my body and anchored itself deeply in my soul. All my muscles squeezed together into a fiercely protective shield. I was terrified.

# Six

What persuades most people is not the
power of logic but the logic of power.
—*Unknown*

From what I could tell, job openings in Tumbleweed were almost nonexistent. Most businesses were owner-operated with few employees. Larger businesses needed people with skills I didn't have. I soon learned that my willingness to do anything and my ability to develop any skill wasn't enough. There were plenty of already trained people who needed work. Getting a job at all was starting to seem uncertain. Getting a stable job might very well be impossible. The whole idea of self-sufficiency started to seem like a wild fantasy. I'd been fired from the first job I could remember—a job where I was earning barely enough to survive. How on earth would I convince anyone to hire me to do anything?

Now I fervently believed that even one misstep, with anyone—at work or outside of work—would take me directly to the street, where I would see just how hideous life as a bag lady could be. Every one of my emotions intensified. They erupted like popcorn and bounced around, passionate and uncontrollable. Prior to every human interaction, panic popped up. I feverishly tried to imagine every possible thing anyone might say or do. I experimented with tone of voice, word choice, facial expressions, and body language. I worked to control my emotions so no one could see how completely inadequate I felt. I endlessly rehearsed everything I could think of to say or do to minimize my chances for failure.

My limited circle of acquaintances had a few suggestions that didn't pan out. Fortunately, before my panic intensified into paralysis, one of them talked to the owner of one of the town's three car dealerships. We scheduled an interview.

In my closet were a few dresses and a couple of suits. I tried each of them on several times. I finally settled on a pink cotton dress that was a touch too big. The skirt had a small, yellowish stain, but I convinced myself it wasn't really noticeable. After I carefully ironed it on my wobbly ironing board, I headed to the interview.

Frank was gnawing on a toothpick while he simultaneously chewed a piece of gum. He smiled, shook my hand, and asked me what I could do. I tried to look confident and capable, but I was sure my spiel was implausible at best. As a result, his job offer took me utterly by surprise. The starting wage was low, but I'd get a twenty-five-cent raise for every month I worked there. I would be replacing the woman who had handled his administrative details for years. I assured him my lack of experience wouldn't be a problem, and that I could learn whatever he needed me to know. He absentmindedly nodded, showed me to my desk, and gave me a few pointers. Then he walked through the showroom to his office, whistling "White Christmas" (the only tune he seemed to know). I was relieved, thrilled, and petrified at the same time. I had a pile of new responsibilities to master.

A true eccentric, Frank had inherited the business from his father. He hadn't seen any need to update anything. His only computer was used to download reports from General Motors on GM-supplied software. Big green ledgers with penciled entries contained all his business accounts. There were just two erasers in the dealership, each zealously hoarded by its user. Frank saved everything—especially paper. Every letter had to be typed on his ancient manual typewriter on the top half of a sheet of business stationery. The bottom half was cut off and carefully stored in a huge cabinet under the counter with other paper of all sizes and colors. Frank had to show me how to roll the paper manually to the next line. I didn't remember how to type, so each letter took far longer than it should have. He didn't seem to mind, as long as it was perfect when he signed it—and as long as it was only half a page long.

Frank patiently answered my endless questions, but his lessons were cursory. He didn't explain things that seemed to be second nature to him: multiplication, debits and credits, check writing, etc. I didn't want anything to jeopardize this job, so I spent hours searching for answers to questions I was afraid to ask. I frantically compared each entry with its corresponding piece of paper and tried to make sense of his system. My mental picture of myself, in tatters and starving, was always close to the surface.

Before I felt comfortable with any aspect of the job, the previous office manager was released from the hospital. Gertrude returned to work and made it clear I was no longer needed. She inspected my ledger entries, grabbed her personal eraser, and started erasing—and grumbling.

"What's wrong?" I asked.

"I'm tired of fixing your mistakes," was her only reply.

That was the first I'd heard of any problems.

"What mistakes?" I asked nervously. She didn't answer.

"Tell me how to fix them," I suggested, "so I won't make them again."

She shook her head, glared at me, and repeated, "I'm tired of fixing your mistakes."

Turning her back to me, she went back to her erasing.

My emotions ratcheted to a new high. Apparently,

Gertrude had never planned on retiring. She didn't need any help. She wasn't interested in training me to do anything. She ignored me. She lambasted me. She refused to give me any work. She obviously wanted me to go away.

Finally, Frank wedged a desk into a tiny space behind the counter for me. I looked for anything to do: washing windows, organizing cupboards, whatever I could find to stay busy and earn my pay. Gertrude seemed to resent everything I did. Whenever I even touched anything, she snarled. With every passing day, my terror increased. *Would this be the day I'd be fired?*

After work, I spent increasing amounts of time outside, running or biking, letting the exercise and fresh air soften the day's blows. During one run, I decided I had to face facts. Prosperity would probably be impossible for me. My half brain and less-than-stellar work record might even keep me from ever finding a decent job. I'd probably always need at least two jobs to meet expenses and to keep money coming in if I lost one. I'd have to work like a demon to keep any job. I'd have to work until I died.

The classified ads in the local paper took two minutes to read each day. One day, an intriguing ad appeared. Somebody was looking for an instructor for a to-be-established karate school for kids. There were three magic words at the end of the ad: "No experience necessary." I looked at the martial arts belts of every color mounted in a frame on my kitchen wall, and thought about the black belt in my closet. I watched a video I'd found of myself, kicking, punching, and yelling during my final black belt test, then raced to the phone and made an appointment.

When I met the owner of the karate school, she instantly recognized me.

"Beki?" she was incredulous. "Don't you remember me? We earned our black belts together!"

Giving me a happy hug, Kelly told me she was recruiting independent contractors to teach self-defense classes. She answered my questions and explained how to handle the money.

Then she pulled out the lesson plans and explained to me, "The classes are primarily safety classes, with advice on how to react appropriately to tornados, fires, potential kidnappers, and bullies. Karate lessons are integral to the classes. Kids love learning karate, and parents appreciate the safety lessons."

I loved the idea. Then she showed me sketches of the moves I'd be teaching. Horrified, I realized I didn't remember any of them. I explained what had happened. Kelly looked confused for a minute, handed me a book full of sketches of people in various positions and gave me some perfunctory lessons in stance and form. The moves weren't as hard as I'd expected. She was convinced I could effortlessly do the job. I agreed that I could probably handle it, but I knew it would take a lot of practice. I cautiously agreed to become an instructor.

I raced home and designed a flyer, flew over to the local print shop, and had a few printed. Frank agreed to let me distribute flyers for my new venture at work. Everyone instantly became a potential customer.

That's how I got to know Ken. Every day, the tall, gangly, curly-headed UPS man made his delivery at the car dealership, with a big smile and a cheery "Hello!" One day, as he waited for a signature, I raced over to the counter.

"Excuse me," I said. "Do you have any kids who might be interested in a karate class?"

His eyes twinkled as he grinned. "I have kids, but they're way too old for karate."

"Do they have kids?" I asked. "Or do you know anyone with kids?"

His kids lived out of town, but he said he might know some people. I was sure he would; he'd probably delivered something to everyone in Tumbleweed. I handed him some flyers. He agreed to give them to anyone who might be even remotely interested.

Fewer than a dozen kids signed up for the first classes. There were two courses, each lasting fourteen weeks. At the end of the first course, each kid earned a yellow belt. They got orange belts when they successfully mastered the more complicated karate moves in the second course.

One day, as Ken made his rounds, he asked how the class was going. I told him about an upcoming session where I would be teaching my kids how to deal with bullies. I needed to find someone to be my bully.

"What does this person have to do?" he asked.

"Well, he just has to act like a bully, so the kids can practice their techniques on him," I explained. Before he could say a word, I had a brilliant idea. Impulsively, I asked, "Would you be interested in being my bully?"

He agreed and I was relieved. That was the beginning of what would prove to be the luckiest acquaintance of my life.

At the end of the second course, I asked Kelly for the next level's curriculum. It didn't exist. I couldn't remember any more karate moves. I couldn't afford to take classes to learn any more, so I couldn't design more advanced classes myself. Disappointed, I decided not to renew the contract. Once again, I was dependent on only one source of income—and my situation at the car dealership hadn't improved.

# Seven

A few weeks later, I had a magnificent stroke of luck. The local call center had just signed a contract to handle incoming technical support calls for a new client. They had some entry-level openings for customer service reps to help callers solve problems with their computer systems and create computer records of those calls. They were hiring anyone who could see lightning, hear thunder, and speak into a phone. They provided a meager benefit package—something I hadn't heard of in Tumbleweed. Best of all, they didn't ask any detailed questions about my skills, and I didn't mention my memory loss.

They offered me a job at the end of the interview; I gave Frank my resignation the next day. Two weeks later, I walked through the front door of one of the newer buildings in town. Again, I was simultaneously relieved and scared stiff. I remembered nothing about computers, and my teaspoon of experience on Frank's ancient typewriter had done little for my typing speed. If I did well, this might be the stable job I was looking for. If I didn't, it would be tough, if not impossible, to find any other job in that small town.

The training class lasted three days. The stack of notebooks and handouts were full of instructions on how to handle each call. They detailed everything from the greeting to the troubleshooting steps to take. The information was clear and simple, but it didn't make much sense to me then. I took my notes home every night and struggled to understand the alien world of operating systems and DOS commands; peripherals, ports, and cables; and the intricacies of the World Wide Web.

Most of my coworkers were in their twenties. Their emotions were almost tangible—and generally negative. They resented being told what to do. They followed instructions only if they felt they had no other choice. When their experience was, for whatever reason, intolerable, a popular comment was, "I was looking for a job when I found this one."

Their attitudes toward customers were equally confusing. Many callers were having problems with the first computer system they'd ever owned. As a result, their questions were pretty basic. According to the experts in the surrounding cubicles, however, everyone should have known the answers to those questions before they were born.

"That guy is so stupid; he shouldn't be allowed to own a computer!"

"I had to tell that idiot where the 'Enter' key was on his keyboard!"

"How hard is it to hold a key down while you start your computer?"

"This jerk forgot to plug his printer in after he moved it, and then wondered why it didn't work. Duh!"

I couldn't understand them. *Would they like to be treated*

*that way when they called someone for help?* I found working with and solving problems for customers quite rewarding. Besides, weren't we being paid to help people learn things they didn't know? *Weren't our customers the people who ultimately paid our salaries?* Maybe my coworkers had never had a hard time finding a job. Maybe they'd never been fired. Or…maybe they knew something I didn't.

The kids' conversations when they weren't on the phone were equally disturbing. They'd gather in the back of the room and talk about who they'd slept with, what had happened at the local bar, or what drugs they'd tried lately.

One day, the guy in the cubicle behind me pushed the "Mute" button on his telephone in the middle of a call, stood up, and yelled, "This guy is a fuckin' shitball!" I was aghast. Everyone else seemed to take the comment in stride; some even chuckled as they continued to talk with their customers.

I decided to speak to my supervisor. She was about thirty years old, with long black hair. Her perpetual scowl and customary black dress made her look like a witch. Her attitude was correspondingly frightening. For days, I rehearsed what to say and tried to imagine every possible reaction she might have to it. I came up with what I hoped was the best response in each case. I just knew that one misstep could put me out on the street. Still, I reasoned that if the kids' comments alienated enough customers, our client companies wouldn't renew their contracts. We needed all the business we could get. Finally, I summoned the courage to walk to her cubicle. When I entered, she looked up, obviously irritated and impatient. Timidly, I asked if it would be okay if I moved to a different desk.

"Why?" she asked.

"Well, I don't really think some of my coworkers' comments are…."

She interrupted me. "Everybody always asks each other

questions about the issue they're trying to resolve. Get used to it."

"Their questions aren't what bother me," I said nervously. "It's what they say about their weekends, the way they talk to the customers, and...."

"Get used to it," she repeated, and turned back to the papers on her desk.

I felt a flood of what I thought had been fundamental truths dissolve as I walked back to my cubicle. As I sat down, the room looked, sounded, and felt like a bizarre, evil spaceship, complete with dark, burgundy lighting. *Was this the way the world really worked? Would I have to learn how to be someone I couldn't respect in order to survive?* After all, my job history so far had been a series of contradictory and nonsensical experiences. *If the world was that alien, would I ever be able to adapt?* Clearly, my instincts about life were fundamentally flawed.

After work, I knocked on my neighbor Vern's door and told him what had happened. He listened impassively, then said, "The boss may not always be right, honey, but she's always the boss."

"But what do I do? I don't know if I can treat the customers the way they do. I don't want to become that kind of person."

Vern just shrugged and shook his head. "That's life, honey."

I changed clothes and went outside for a run. I knew I couldn't support myself if I didn't understand how the world really worked. At the same time, I didn't know how I could force myself to consistently do things that demeaned or damaged everyone involved. People outside work kept telling me, "Just be yourself." *Right!* My current "self" had to be a twisted version of the person I thought I used to be. That person had been successful; she'd fit into this extraterrestrial world. The person I was now was an actor without a script in a terrifying science fiction movie. *If my concept of right and wrong differed so fundamentally from that of the rest of the world, would it even be possible for me to learn how to behave appropriately?* I finally realized I didn't have the luxury of choice. If I was to survive, I'd have to learn to behave appropriately, no matter how repulsive that might be.

I was now absolutely convinced that one misstep with anyone at work, and probably outside of work, could get me fired. I couldn't ask my young coworkers for advice; they seemed to feel I was a clueless old woman beyond help. I'd have to figure it out myself, but I couldn't even imagine how I was going to do that. I started scrutinizing the way everyone interacted with each other like some zoologist in a troop of orangutans. Every evening, on my rickety living room couch, I breathed a sigh of relief. I still had a job. With each experience, however, I became increasingly confused, frustrated, and scared. I wasn't sure how long I'd be able to postpone inevitable disaster.

# Eight

Life is the art of drawing sufficient conclusions from insufficient premises.

—*Samuel Butler*

I frantically searched for direction. My fellow humans were always baffling, mostly frightening creatures. They seemed to expect things of me: actions or reactions I must have understood before my knowledge of them evaporated. I had no way of knowing that my behaviors were unremarkable and, for the most part, appropriate. I believed that, clueless as I was, I had to be acting strangely. How could I stay employed if I couldn't rely on my instincts? I wouldn't be able to keep any job, much less ever get a decent one, unless I knew how I was expected to act.

I wished people were like nature. Nature made sense. If you looked hard enough, you could discover why anything happened—from the activities of a spider to the changes in the weather. I'd never thought of people as part of nature. After all, they lived in structures that separated them from nature. They seemed to be intent on controlling it, when they weren't ignoring it.

One day, however, the answer materialized. I realized that whether they thought so or not, humans *were* creatures of nature. From what I'd learned, the world had always been a hazardous place for humans. Survival of the species probably wouldn't have been possible if they hadn't banded together for mutual protection. Within their communities, behaviors that put everyone at risk were surely discouraged. As communities evolved into societies, a sort of behavior code undoubtedly developed and trickled down through the generations. With each generation, those "Laws of Life" (as I named the code) would have become more deeply etched into the communal conscience. Eventually, those subconscious laws became governors of human behavior as surely as the law of gravity governs physical movement in our galaxy. It was only logical.

What a relief! *Human behavior could be scientifically explained and eventually understood!* The people in this small, mostly peaceful town seemed to support this theory. Everyone seemed to be comfortable with themselves and their place in the world. For the most part, they seemed to get along. If I could somehow identify the Laws of Life, I'd be able to understand how to behave appropriately in my world. Once I knew how to act, I could figure out how to survive. I had to discover those laws.

I'd scrimped and saved for months before I could afford to take the introductory cell biology class at the local junior college. One of the first lectures discussed the scientific method. As I understood it, scientists proposed a hypothesis to explain a phenomenon. Then they tested it. If it survived their tests, it was accepted as a theory. That theory may last years or decades or days. It could be abandoned at any time, in light of new evidence, and replaced with a new, more accurate hypothesis.

Since the scientific method had helped make sense of the infinitely intricate processes of nature, I thought that it could help me identify those Laws of Life which defined appropriate human behavior. I would accumulate information from experiences, experimentation, observation, and study. I would get ideas and advice from every resource I could find. I would dissect and analyze every bit of that information to identify the Law of Life that explained it. I would use future experiences and discoveries to help me validate or disprove my deductions. All the facts, ideas, and understanding I accumulated would become my database of knowledge. Eventually, that database would include all the Laws of Life. I would understand human behavior. That understanding would make it possible for me to become an accepted, self-sufficient member of my world.

Until I knew the Laws of Life, there was always a very real possibility that I would behave so inappropriately that I would end up hopelessly unemployed, or worse. Uncovering those laws wouldn't be just a philosophical field trip—my survival would depend on it.

# Nine

Now that I had a plan, I needed a strategy. Ever since Dad told me that people love questions, I'd peppered everyone I met with all kinds of questions. When it came to questions about appropriate behavior, however, I was starting to see a major problem. Recently, my sister had told me that, in my prior life, she had become impatient with our endless discussions about my various problems. She added that her husband had sworn off giving me advice about anything.

When I heard that, I was stunned. Dad had never even hinted that some kinds of questions might not be welcome. I had to find another way to learn about appropriate behavior. Observation seemed relatively risk free, so I watched everyone around me until I came up with a theoretical law. Then, I watched everyone around me again, scrutinizing every nuance of each word, expression, and gesture to prove its validity. I found a few people who didn't seem to mind answering questions, and I asked them if the behavior I had observed was universal.

Looking back, it's hard to remember all the theoretical laws I came up with. Most were so fleeting I don't recall them at all. For example, if someone looked at me when we passed on the street, I theorized that people always looked up when they approached someone else. When the next person I passed didn't look up, I took that theory off the Law list.

Sometimes people gave me what I thought was a full-blown Law. My dad told me that men always open doors for women. "It's a way to show respect," he explained. "In turn, women show respect for men by waiting for them to open doors for them." That law was disproved the day after he gave it to me. None of the guys I worked with opened the door for anyone but themselves.

In any case, it never took long for someone to break one of my theoretical laws. *There goes that theory* soon became my mantra. My experiences with people got more confusing by the day, and my inability to understand them made me feel vulnerable and scared. I couldn't avoid everyone, but how could I get anyone to accept me if I didn't know how to act?

I asked my dad for advice. He suggested that the first step to acceptance was a smile and a cheerful greeting.

"I hardly know anyone," I told him. "Won't they think I'm being weird?"

"You don't have to know them," he assured me. "They're your neighbors. You're just saying, 'Hi.'"

It was worth a shot. I started to smile and wave at anyone I passed on the street, consciously scattering sunshine. Hopefully, this would open some doors for me, without scaring everyone away.

My neighbor, Vern (that old grump) disapproved. He told me I shouldn't wave and smile at men. He said that I was "prostituting" myself. How ridiculous was that! My old clothes were far from sexy, and I certainly wasn't trying to wave and smile provocatively. Vern was a jaded old loner, I concluded. As a former state patrolman, maybe he had only seen people at their worst. It didn't matter. I knew that everyone, including men, had to be governed by the same Laws of Life.

Besides, for a while, nearly all the people in my life were men. Friendships with women had scared me ever since I could remember. I wasn't sure why. The women I'd met so far didn't seem to be particularly friendly, and my relationships at work had led me to believe that they were insensitive, competitive, and ruthless. Maybe my instincts were based on forgotten past experiences. After all, my sisters mentioned that I had suspected infidelity in my previous marriages. Whatever the case might be, I saw no reason to go out of my way to make friends with women.

Men, on the other hand, cropped up everywhere. Single, divorced, separated, widowed—even married—they all seemed to have a lot of time on their hands. They seemed eager to get to know me, and I was comfortable with most of them. When they complimented me on my beauty, I dismissed their remarks. I told them that I didn't have any control over the genes my mother and father had given me. Besides, I thought I was quite average looking. On the other hand, their compliments on things like my sense of humor, or my ability to "tell it like it is," told me I was learning at least a few things about how to be appropriate. Men were more than willing to answer any question I came up with. They seemed to dismiss my memory loss and my epilepsy as trivial, which was an atypical, welcome response to my situation.

Best of all, men seemed to be looking for the same thing I was: friends, not mates. The married men who approached me weren't considering divorce, but none of them had anything good to say about their wives, either. I heard all kinds of miserable stories about one failed relationship after another. I was soon convinced that an impressive pile of mysterious, intricate, almost superhuman skills must be required to make a relationship last. Evidently, I hadn't been very good at it before I lost my memory. I'd been divorced three times, after decades of life experience!

My now-tiny bag of experiences gave me very few clues to love's forgotten secrets. Committed relationships seemed to be mazes with no exit. To me, they were as unappealing as they were out of reach. Besides, I didn't have another forty-seven years to learn what I used to know.

Unquestionably, friendship with unmarried males was my best option. Friendship was straightforward and uncomplicated. Honesty was its foundation. Freedom was its heart. Friends didn't see each other through a haze of hormones. Their emotions didn't leap between jealousy and elation. They didn't pout if their friends acted unpredictably. They didn't run away, heartbroken, when times got tough and the storybook turned into reality. Friendship didn't limit growth. Friends were free to grow in different directions without restricting or binding each other. Friendships could survive time and distance.

Sex seemed to be a natural part of friendship with a man. It was a topic every man quickly broached. I still had a fair supply of hormones; sex was clearly a natural impulse—a harmless, healthy desire. I was also sure it was something friends could share. The men I met agreed.

Again, my opinionated neighbor objected. Vern felt strongly that sex could be one of the most destructive of human impulses. Try as I might, however, I couldn't see a downside to a natural physical expression of friendship. When he realized we weren't going to agree, he asked me if I at least understood the risks of having sex.

It hadn't occurred to me that sex might be risky. I didn't know much about the reproductive process at all. I learned about menstruation one day when I started bleeding at work. I thought I was hemorrhaging and raced to the local emergency room. What I learned there was confusing. I couldn't remember ever having a period. Back at home, I searched my medical records and learned that I hadn't had one for the last several years.

Vern expanded on the brief explanation I'd been given at the hospital. He explained the facts of life and stressed the importance of contraceptives. I was offended at Vern's suggestion that I might date a lowlife with some disease, but I knew I didn't want children. Men didn't raise serious objections to contraception. Some even assured me they'd been "fixed." Naturally, I believed them. Fortunately, very few of my "friendships" lasted long enough to become passionate.

By that time, Ken had taken me out on a few dates. We had had sex. What was a natural expression of friendship for me started to seem like much more to Ken. I kept explaining why I believed a good friend was infinitely more valuable than an exclusive partner. Like all the other men, he kept saying he agreed. Even so, he got jealous whenever I even spoke a male-sounding name. He started to bring me a rose every day when he made his delivery. That made me uncomfortable, but he assured me that flowers were just a traditional expression of friendship.

Every time a man took me out, I analyzed our time together for clues to the Laws of Life. Why did he react that way? What did that look mean? Why did he use that tone of voice? Why did he use that word, that gesture? I read books, too. Author after author explained how different men were from women and how difficult it was for each to understand the other. As soon as I came up with a hypothetical Law, the next man's behavior disproved it.

The possibility that men's motives for relationships might be different than mine didn't occur to me. Maybe I just didn't "speak their language." All I knew was that identifying the Laws of Life regarding relationships with men was going to be more difficult than I had assumed. The more men I met, the less faith I had in my ability to find even one of those laws.

Eventually, I decided that relationships would take more time than I could spare right then. They were too mercurial. Maybe someday I could explore one or two. Until then, I needed to focus on the practical aspects of life. The challenge of unraveling male mysteries would have to wait until I reached my goal of financial stability. Discovering the Laws of Life at the same time that I was learning to support myself would be tricky enough all by itself.

# Ten

Certainly the same man. Questionably the same person.

—*John Locke*

I felt like a bad fisherman must feel. I kept casting my line without catching anything. The harder I struggled, the more elusive those keys to behavior seemed. How had everyone else learned everything they knew?

Of course, I knew about schools. I wasn't sure exactly what was taught there, but I figured it must be pretty comprehensive, since college degrees were required for so many jobs. One of the most important learning resources, however, was one I didn't even recognize at first: families.

I didn't know what to think about families. Maybe they were simply population boosters. I knew they usually included a mother, father, and kids. I assumed the parents took care of the kids until they were able to take care of themselves. When they moved out, I assumed they shook hands and went their separate ways. Any relationship after that surely would take the shape of other adult associations.

People around me, however, seemed to feel that relationships between family members were somehow different than those with others. Many times, when I turned to people for advice or support, they asked me if I'd talked to my family. I didn't really understand why anyone would rely on family members more than on others in their world.

As a result, I wasn't sure how to act with my family. Each of them was willing to answer my questions and give me advice, but I didn't consider them to be more credible or reliable than anyone else. After all, I didn't know them as well as the people I knew in Tumbleweed.

When holidays came around, everyone assumed I'd be spending them with my family. As a result, in the beginning, I spoke with or visited my family frequently. My sisters Melissa and Lindsay now lived in the same town. As I got to know them and their families, I became more confused. We were all very different from each other. I didn't understand how that was possible, since the three of us had the same parents and we'd spent our childhoods together. I wasn't sure how I was supposed to act as a sister, so the two-hour trip to visit Lindsay and Melissa was always stressful. (To make matters worse, my little Jetta was getting old, and it was starting to blow fuses in quaint, remote spots.) However, by the end of each weekend, I'd think about the fun I'd had and the unique connection I'd started to feel.

That connection seemed to come with some kind of mutual support that couldn't be found anywhere else. Since I couldn't imagine the kinds of experiences families shared, evidence of that connection always surprised me. For example, one day I opened my mail to discover a huge credit card bill. I couldn't imagine why I'd ever decided to buy over ten thousand dollars worth of stuff on credit. In a total panic, I told my dad about my discovery. Immediately, he offered to mortgage his house and loan me more than two-thirds of my annual income without a written agreement. I was as surprised as I was grateful. Everyone else acted almost nonchalant, like that was the kind of thing family members always did for each other.

As time went on, my dad's visits showed me another

facet of family membership. Every now and then, he'd travel out west to see "his girls," as he called me and my sisters. He'd schedule a block of time for us to spend together. We'd discuss everything from philosophies, politics, and current events to what was happening to me. He taught me more about life in those discussions than most people probably learn in a lifetime of schooling. I was more grateful than he'll probably ever know, but he acted like it was something fathers did all the time for their children.

My baby sister, Melissa, and her family gave me something else to think about. One day, as I was weeding my minigarden, she and her family drove up unexpectedly and parked behind my Jetta.

"We're going to the big city, Beki," they announced. "Do you want to come along?"

I was as delighted with the invitation as I was surprised by it, but I was covered with dirt. I ran upstairs for the speediest shower in history and raced to the car. The trip turned out to be just one of many visits filled with laughter. After that, whenever I needed to feel better about myself and my world, I reached for the phone and called Melissa.

As time went on, each member of my family was encouraging. They told me that with good ideas and hard work, I could achieve whatever goals I set for myself. Their experiences were vivid examples, for me, of the good and bad consequences of various behaviors, beliefs, and approaches to life. They related the history of our pioneering ancestors to illustrate what could be accomplished with clear vision, courage, and persistence. They came up with all kinds of ideas to help me create a viable future. They encouraged me to succeed, and they assured me I would. With every positive experience, I felt like I was the luckiest person in the world. I had a wonderful family that cared about me and was willing to be there whenever I needed someone. I still didn't really know what "family" meant, but my dad, stepmother, sisters, brothers-in-law, nieces, and nephews were some of the best people I knew.

Then, without fail, something would happen or be said that seemed to contradict that perception. For example, when I asked my sisters about our childhood together, the stories they told were generally about some traumatic event we'd shared. In contrast, Ken's stories about his childhood were almost always about the fun he'd had growing up. After a while, I concluded that our childhood must have been all business. I wondered how much fun we'd really had.

When I asked specifically about the kind of person I'd been, the feedback was also discouraging. My sisters said I'd been a strong-willed crusader who'd tried to recruit them for idealistic battles that didn't interest them in the least. They seemed to believe I was someone who fought for attention by getting into trouble. They said I had a hot temper and sometimes said things that still hurt them. I was the only one who had threatened to move out during an argument with Dad. I was the only one who had been divorced; my multiple divorces made that failing even worse. My father told me I was a member of the "hippie generation," a bunch of dope heads who had destroyed everything decent in society. Maybe I'd absorbed that despicable hippie mentality to an unacceptable degree. It sounded like I hadn't been fun to live with, at best.

When I asked my college roommate for her perspective, she described a completely different person. She said we'd always had a lot of harmless fun together eating pizza, listening to music in the college "listening room," and playing Frisbee in a tiny park in the middle of town. She said I'd refused to even experiment with drugs. She wasn't aware of any problems I'd had with my family. I wasn't sure who to believe. (After all, my roommate was a member of the hippie generation, too.)

When I asked my family about my life after the seizures started, none of them gave me any solid information. They answered most of my questions, but some of their answers seemed evasive and guarded. As I felt my way through conversations, things were often said that convinced me I'd said or done something to alienate me from them. For example, one thing I heard from everyone is that after I'd lost my job, I asked if I could move in with one of them until I got my feet on the ground. They all refused, for varying reasons. My dad and one of my sisters told me they'd spoken to professional counselors, who advised a dose of tough love (whatever that was). They all added that, after their decision, I continually reminded them of how much their refusals had hurt.

I wasn't sure how I was supposed to feel. I didn't have any solid information to go on. It sounded like the person I'd been and the way I'd reacted to life before had been ineffective at best and damaging at worst. I couldn't relate to what they said happened; I couldn't imagine ever asking to move in with anyone. It was hard to know how to apologize for something that may or may not have been justified, in my mind, at the time. I didn't really know these people who claimed to know me so well. As a result, I didn't really feel much about any of them, one way or the other. I decided the best thing for me to do would be to disappear from their lives and put them out of their misery.

To test that theory, I decided not to initiate any contact, to see what they'd do. Sometimes months would pass before I heard from anyone. I received invitations to family gatherings just before the events, and I wasn't included in the preparations. I must have been right; I had somehow irreparably damaged our relationships.

Inevitably, whenever I came to that conclusion, one of them would call and ask how things were going. I felt uncomfortable discussing my latest dilemma, but they generally kept asking questions until I started to wonder if they might really be interested. Finally, I asked my sisters to have lunch with me at a café during my next visit.

After we ordered, I took a deep breath. "I'm really confused. Ever since my seizures stopped, I've gotten the impression that I must have done something in the past to damage our relationships. It seems like you include me in family events out of obligation, not because you really want me to be there. If that's true, I'd appreciate knowing that."

"Beki, you're our sister. No matter what you do, we'll always love you," they said.

"I appreciate that," I said. "But I can't remember what happened. I'd rather be excluded from the family than included out of a sense of duty."

"You don't understand. We've shared a lifetime of experiences, good and bad. Nothing can change that. You'll always be a part of our family."

The conversation was frustrating. Neither sister had answered my question. In fact, their statements convinced me I was right. Whatever I'd done apparently wasn't positive. It was something they'd never forget, and it was something they didn't seem to want to talk about. Maybe one of the Laws of Life was that family members had to treat each other differently than they treated everyone else. Maybe they weren't supposed to slam the door on a family member, even if she deserved it.

Even though my relationships with my extended family have deepened over the last nine years, I'm still not sure what families are all about. I can only try to imagine the kinds of things people learn just from being a member of a family. I'll always wonder if my discomfort with my own family was justified, or if it was just impossible for me to imagine how people and relationships can change over the course of a lifetime. All I know is that my life with my family has been far shorter than the one they remember with me. I'll always wonder if they'll ever recognize me as the person I am now: someone who can never truly be the person they used to know.

# Eleven

Man will occasionally stumble over the truth, but most of the time he will pick himself up and continue on.
—*Winston Churchill*

My search for the Laws of Life was still my top priority. However, I'd had to take it underground. No one seemed to understand what I was looking for. When I explained my theory about the evolution of a set of ingrained laws, people generally nodded slowly before they replied. Some denied the existence of any such laws. Others seemed to talk around the question without really answering it. However, as unproductive as those discussions were to my quest, they provided me with some invaluable coping tools.

For example, years ago, my sister Lindsay had started a consulting business. She designed seminars based on a psychological tool to help people live harmoniously and work effectively together. Theoretically, everyone has a multitude of instincts that drive them from within, and everyone fundamentally prefers some instincts over others. If we know each individual's personality preferences, we can use that knowledge to harmoniously achieve our mutual goals.

We spent months discussing those various preferences. We talked about all kinds of people in various situations, real and imagined. The information gave me feasible explanations for why people acted the way they did. It gave me possible reasons for my feelings of estrangement from society other than my lack of a past. She told me the ways I interpreted the world and interacted with people may have made me seem intimidating, aloof, and overly confident. The information made sense, and it helped me develop a few tentative relationships. Because it dealt with individuals, however, the tool obviously didn't penetrate deeply enough into our consciousness to identify the fundamental laws I was still sure everyone in a society shared.

Another place where I picked up some coping tools was at a local chapter of Alcoholics Anonymous (AA). Ever since I could remember, I'd been a member of AA. After my last seizure, I couldn't remember why I'd joined. A fellow member recounted a story I'd told at my first meeting, a story I later confirmed using my medical records.

Before I moved to Tumbleweed, I was living in a small town about thirty miles away. I was working for one of Dad's friends, a heavy equipment manufacturer. One night, the biggest blizzard of the year roared into the area. Sometime after midnight, I was found, coatless and unconscious, on an overpass and rushed to the hospital. My father flew to the hospital from Washington DC. The doctors told him that, by the time I was found, I had no more than ten minutes of life left. My blood alcohol was high, and the policeman recommended that I join Alcoholics Anonymous. My dad's trip across country shook me so badly that I agreed. Maybe I was an alcoholic.

It is only recently that I started to wonder if I might have had a partial seizure that night that no one recognized. The "drunken" incident had happened in the middle of the night, around the time I normally had seizures. According to the Epilepsy Foundation, "Lack of public understanding has led to people with complex partial seizures being unfairly arrested as drunk or disorderly, or being accused by others of…drug abuse—all because of actions produced by seizures." It's possible that I'd had a seizure in a bar ending with a walk into the freezing storm. Although alcohol undoubtedly hadn't helped, epilepsy might have been the primary reason for that blackout.

A few other incidents support that theory. On a trip to Lindsay's house, my sister said I'd been brought home by a stranger after I woke up in my nightshirt several blocks from her house. Another time, a neighbor in Tumbleweed stopped me and asked if I was OK. She'd seen me walking down the street in the middle of the night in my pajamas, oblivious to the world around me.

From friends, family, and my medical records, I know that alcohol was part of my life before my seizures stopped. Since that last seizure, I've tried various kinds of drinks. Today, I occasionally enjoy a glass of wine with a steak dinner, but I have no desire to keep drinking after the meal. For the most part, liquor seems to be a pretty good waste of money.

That night on the overpass, however, alcohol did me a favor. Joining AA turned out to be one of the best things I ever did. It was there that I got to really know Hank, the tall, thin gentleman I'd met before my last seizure. Hank had grown up on a farm and had known my dad. His smiles were rare and restrained, but his eyes sparkled when something tickled him. Whenever I excitedly told him of my latest discovery, he listened with a bemused look. He'd obviously known for some time what I'd just learned. He was the first person I felt I could talk freely with. After a few discussions, I was sure he knew the Laws of Life. When I asked him about them, however, he said there were no such laws.

That answer was discouraging, but I thought about it. Maybe the laws were so deeply ingrained that they were consciously unrecognizable. Perhaps the laws I was looking for were like whatever laws or instincts made even abandoned cats clean their faces and paws after eating. Many, if not all, of the Laws of Life that dictated human behavior were probably, by their very nature, subconscious.

One of the longest-standing members in the local chapter, Hank had been sober for more than twenty years. He believed in attending as many meetings as possible. I couldn't understand his devotion, but I didn't object to his insistence that I go with him at least once a week. As a clueless floater in a river of experienced navigators, I hoped I could decipher some laws by observing other members.

The meetings didn't help me clearly identify any laws either, but they were priceless. I learned that we constantly make choices that impact our lives and relationships. As everyone related their experiences, I had a chance to witness the consequences of various choices. Members discussed the things that had happened to them and how they had reacted. They gave me a tool chest full of effective responses to a myriad of situations. Their advice helped me cope with a chaotic, overwhelming world and prepare for an unknowable, terrifying future.

The serenity prayer was probably their most valuable gift. A shortened variation of a prayer written in the 1940s by Reinhold Niebuhr, it went: "God, grant me the serenity to accept the things I cannot change, the courage to change the things I can, and the wisdom to know the difference." It became a mantra I endlessly repeated as I tried to react appropriately to the multitude of situations I faced every day.

"Grant me the serenity to accept the things I cannot change." The key word in the opening phrase was "serenity." Acceptance wasn't a problem for me then. I didn't have a past. That was a fact. I didn't understand the world enough to see what kinds of things I could choose not to accept. Another fact: I had to be the sole cause of any hiccups or failures in every one of my interactions, since everyone else already knew the score. Every time I relived my latest mess in detail, Hank repeatedly said, "Don't beat yourself up." I didn't understand why he thought I was beating myself up. I was just reviewing everything, trying to spot the mistakes I'd made. It was the only way I could avoid making them again in the future. In light of these "facts," serenity was hard to come by.

"[T]he courage to change the things I can" was more difficult. Since I hadn't seen much of the outside world, I didn't know what things I should try to change. Besides, the few minor changes I'd suggested had already cost me one job. Who knows what other havoc I could courageously create? The only changes I could make now were internal. Courageous or not, I had to learn what behaviors were appropriate if I wanted to survive. Then, and only then, would I be able to start to consider the possibility of changing anything else.

"And the wisdom to know the difference" seemed impossible at that time. Mushrooms were wiser that I was. At least a mushroom knew how to stay alive. Sometimes I wondered if I'd ever know that much.

Fellow members encouraged me to explore spiritual alternatives. I went to Christian churches, experimented with Buddhism, and read books and literature supplied by devout door-to-door believers. None of the doctrines did much for me. In fact, missionaries' apparently insatiable desire to convince everyone of their exclusive ability to connect with a creator seemed arrogant, intrusive, and hypocritical. Many of the things they preached, like the Golden Rule, they didn't always practice. I concluded that religious beliefs and philosophies were merely suggestions for ways to make life easier. They couldn't be Laws of Life. Just as we couldn't choose to ignore the physical law of gravity, we were helpless to behave in ways other than those defined by the Laws of Life.

Other ways to cope seemed to come naturally. For example, a run or a bike ride under the magnificent, ever-changing sky never failed to calm me and renew my flimsy faith in myself. Nature gave me the sense of peace, awe, and inexplicable optimism many people described when they spoke of their faith. The part of the world without people in it was still a wonderful place. Whenever I could, I escaped from the hazardous world of unpredictable humans to experience more of the real world, the world where people lived, but didn't truly belong.

Music was another powerful companion. Whether it was music I already knew or music I discovered, each artist reacquainted me with some of the things I probably used to know, or needed to know, about life. Their words gave me their perspectives. Their music cradled my heart. Music was my constant companion and old friend. It allowed me to feel and express emotions I could experience nowhere else. Its overwhelming beauty gave me a sense of belonging in an alien, threatening world. I'm not sure how I could have lived without it.

I was also determined to make my life fun. A lifetime of experiences had been stolen from me. I was determined to enjoy as much of the rest of my life as I could. Whether I was outside by myself or inside with people, I tried to find something to feel good about.

All these coping tools were helpful, but my journey was still frustrating. I was more convinced than ever that the key to success with people lay in finding the Laws of Life, those subconscious, built-in laws of appropriate behavior. When would I start identifying any of them?

# Twelve

One day, to my amazement, I realized I'd been working at the call center for two years. I was semicomfortable with my job skills, but I still felt far from stable. My job was the best I could land in this town, and I was still barely earning enough to survive. I volunteered for as much overtime as I could get at work, and I appreciated the extra money.

I also looked for part-time ways to earn money. I checked on food stamps, but I wasn't eligible because I was working. I called the local Army recruiter, and I learned that I was too old to enlist. I answered an ad offering to buy unfertilized eggs for in vitro fertilization, for up to five thousand dollars, but, again, I was too old. I looked into selling my blood, but the closest facility was two hours away.

Ken was then living with a shattered heel. He had fallen from a tree, trying to rescue a cat. He had to have repeated corrective surgeries over the next few years. Between trips to the hospital, he hobbled around on crutches. An ex-Marine, he wanted to live in a spotless home, but he swore he'd "rather take a beating than clean." He wasn't happy with his current cleaning lady, but he couldn't find another one. I immediately volunteered to take her place. I also offered

to mow his lawn for free, if he'd show me how to do it. (I
liked the idea of working outside, and I thought I might be
able to earn some money mowing lawns.)

Even with all the extra pennies I collected, I was keeping
just enough in my checking account to cover my most basic
expenses. One day as Hank walked me home from work, I
told him I didn't know how I could survive on my minimal
income.

"Live within your means," was his terse reply.

I was puzzled. "What do you mean?"

He was uncompromising. "Live within your means."

"But, how do…?" I started to ask again. Uncharacteris-
tically, he turned and walked across the street toward his
little home.

Back in my apartment, I thought about Hank's answer.
He'd spent most of his life working in the oil fields and had
lived through the Great Depression. If he'd been able to live
within his means, I should surely be able to figure it out.

I pulled out my checkbook. I found some blank paper
and a pencil. I sat down and acted like I knew what to do.
After some thought, I decided to see how I'd been spending
my money. From my checkbook and my pile of receipts, I
made a list of things I'd spent money on. My rent was two
hundred dollars—a huge chunk of my wages. My portion
of my company's health insurance premium was another
sizeable chunk. I didn't have a car payment, but everything I spent on the little heap took more chunks. The only
clothing I'd bought was a pair of dress shoes for work. Very
few of my purchases could be said to be frivolous. My situation looked grim. However, Hank's words rattled around
in my skull. Since I couldn't see how I could consistently
earn more money, I'd just have to come up with ways to
spend less.

I went back through the receipts and checks. I looked
at everything I'd bought and asked myself, *Was that really*

*necessary?* Finally, I had a list of things I didn't need for survival, things like potato chips and dip, houseplants, and video rentals. With the list, I decided to go on spending diets. One of the first was my gas diet. The town was small enough that I could walk or ride my bike anywhere I needed to go. I used my car only when I had to drive long distances or haul something that was too big for my old backpack.

For my utilities diet, I turned down the thermostat in the winter and wore long johns at home. My cash diet required me to write a check whenever I spent anything, giving me a chance to ask, "Is this *really* necessary?" I didn't shop for anything but food.

I brutally justified every expense. For example, trips to visit my sisters were acceptable only because the money I spent on gas would be offset by what I'd save on meals while I was there. Entertainment that cost money, like cable TV or rented movies, were huge extravagances I simply couldn't justify. I'd have to figure out what I could do for fun, for free. At first, I didn't think that would be possible.

When I whined to my dad, he was unsympathetic. "Boredom is an insult to your intelligence," he told me. Well, nobody was going to call me stupid! If there was nothing interesting on TV, I read books or listened to music. I went for runs or scenic bike tours. The most frequent complaint I heard in that small town was that there was nothing to do. I was surprised to read in the local newspaper that something was always going on there: high school basketball games, parades, livestock sales, quarter horse competitions, or farmers' markets. I decided that boredom was just a lame way to justify laziness or self-pity. As an excuse, it could limit our exploration of our world. As a positive force, it could motivate us to learn about it.

It worked, and I learned how to live within my means. As long as everything went well, I was OK. But whenever unplanned expenses like car repairs cropped up, I realized how precarious my finances were. I didn't have any kind of financial cushion to handle emergencies. Possibilities for advancement in my job were remote. I still worried that I might do or say something to get myself fired, or evicted. I'd be lucky if I could ever create more than a meager existence.

# Thirteen

---

The little reed, bending to the force of the wind, soon stood upright again when the storm had passed over.

—*Aesop*

---

I believe that intelligence is our ability to adapt to the world and learn to survive. Memory is a tool that gives us a base of knowledge. We can choose to use memory to increase our chances of survival. We can choose to use it to improve the quality of our lives. However, if we choose not to use it fully—or if we lose some of it—we're still intelligent, we're just not as effective as we could be.

Throughout my short life, I'd been around people who seemed to equate my nonexistent memory with a lack of intelligence or a mental disability. Their attitude was puzzling; they didn't see babies as disabled unless their learning ability was impaired. I'd never felt disabled. I guessed that their viewpoint was the only way those people could get their minds around my situation.

As I walked home from work one evening, I started to wonder if they might be right after all. Maybe my brain had been damaged more than I thought. Maybe I'd lost more than my memory. Until then, I'd been sure I could keep learning until I could create financial stability. As long as I believed that, I could put up with almost anything. But what if I wasn't capable of learning any more? Was I doomed to a life of struggle? Was success completely out of reach? Was I trapped by my ignorance?

I took my questions to my sister, Lindsay, and asked her if she had any ideas for ways I could discover exactly how extensive my brain damage was. She told me about the GED, a test that measures high school students' academic skills. It sounded perfect. I could measure what I knew against the kinds of things people needed to know to get a high school diploma. Maybe I knew more than just how to read and write. At the least, it should show me the kinds of things I needed to know to compete with high school graduates. I marched down to the high school and asked to sign up for the next GED test. My request was refused because I already had a high school degree. I pummeled them with logical arguments, and spiced my request with downright begging. Finally, they gave up and agreed to let me take the pre-GED test.

While I waited for the results, my sister Melissa suggested I take an ACT test at the local junior college. She explained that it was a college entrance exam that measured skills in English, mathematics, reading, science, and writing. The registrars didn't care that I had a bachelor's degree; they took my money and signed me up for the next test.

On both tests, I scored poorly in math, science, and history—things that required recalling facts or details. However, my answers to questions that measured ability to read, understand, and write gave me very high scores. The test results were encouraging, but they didn't completely answer my question. The final step of the learning process is building on the information you've read, understood, and stored in your memory. I still didn't know if my learning had limits. Was I physically capable of learning more?

At Lindsay's recommendations, I visited the local vocational rehabilitation center to see if I might qualify for an education grant. I argued that if I could get a degree I could remember, I should be able to get a better job. After several meetings with the counselor, she told me that since I was employed, she couldn't help me. I tried everything I could think of to change her mind. I promised I would work harder than any other human being on the planet. I assured her the state would be making a good investment, since with a better job, I'd pay more taxes. My arguments didn't work.

A week or so after I'd gotten the ACT test results, the counselor called. She told me she'd received approval for funds to pay for a consultation with a neurophysiologist. He would give me a series of tests to help identify any brain damage. It wasn't an education grant, but it might be a way for me to understand how hopeless my condition really was.

The tests the doctor gave me were interesting and fun. I compared shapes, fitted colored blocks together, interpreted various drawings, and completed wooden jigsaw puzzles blindfolded. Afterward, the doctor explained the test results to me. He told me my ability to learn hadn't been damaged. My brain was healthy and strong. It was just missing a lot of old data. I was intelligent; I had just lost some details. I couldn't have wished for more. I wasn't trapped! It might take a little longer than I had believed at first, but it was still possible to learn how the world worked.

# Fourteen

The next four years were the most tumultuous of my ride to date. They made the first two seem like the slow-moving Mississippi. I think of them, now, as my teenage years.

The few friends I'd made were men. Women didn't seem particularly interested in getting to know me, but men responded quickly to my "sunshine spreading." At that time, it didn't occur to me that my approach to people might not be appropriate. After all, my expert on human behavior (my dad) had told me everyone was fundamentally alike. I couldn't know that effective behavior for a man in the political arena might not produce the same positive results for a woman in the world where most people lived. I assumed that honesty was just one of the many facets of human nature. It didn't occur to me that the people I met might want anything different than what they said they wanted. The term "hidden motives" applied only to hardened criminals or social deviates, I thought. It certainly didn't apply to anyone I was likely to meet.

The men who'd come into my life so far had been interesting but disappointing. Every now and then, I would meet someone who shared one or two of my interests, but, for the most part, we had little in common. After two or three dates, they usually said or did something that convinced me I didn't want to spend any more time with them. For example, one of my would-be friends told me he'd had a near-death experience after he was electrocuted at work. Since then, he'd never seen the moon the way everyone else did. His moon had a diamond crystal hanging from the bottom of it, and a heart hanging from the crystal. He also claimed that he must have absorbed some kind of strange energy, since a particular streetlight went out whenever he drove under it. I was astounded. The world really was stranger than fiction!

Our relationship ended the second time he was two hours late for a dinner date. As I waited, I tried to understand what was happening. Courtesy, something that had seemed to be an undeniable Law of Life, was apparently just another hypothesis. I rehearsed several different ways to approach him with my dilemma. After we ate, I took a deep breath and hesitantly asked him if he could call if it looked like he might be late in the future. Instead of answering, he firmly told me that it was time to drive me home. I tried to get him to answer my question, or at least discuss it. He got up and walked to the cash register. While he was sorting out his money, I decided I didn't want to date anyone who didn't keep his word. I was wearing my running shoes. I rushed out the door and ran all the way home. We didn't date any more.

I finally decided my way of making friends didn't work. I was starting to wonder if I'd be able to make friends with anyone. Everyone else obviously knew something I didn't know. Girls at work were always buzzing about the superhunks they'd met on the Internet, so I decided to try it. Surely, there were one or two guys somewhere who believed as I did: that a solid friendship was something to treasure. Maybe I could build a decent friendship with a pen pal, especially if our chances of actually meeting were rare.

It didn't take long before I met a couple of men who seemed to know what I meant by "nonexclusive friendship." Greg lived three hours from Tumbleweed. He worked from home for an insurance company, maintaining their website. He loved to hike; travel; and read and talk about ideas, scientific discoveries, and history. He'd been a member of a jazz band, and he still owned a grand piano. He'd been looking for a pen pal ever since his last relationship ended painfully. Every day, I looked forward to his email. I'd finally met someone I could really talk to.

Chuck lived in Oklahoma, so we'd probably never meet in person either. He had a great sense of humor, and his emails were sprinkled with southern sayings. The things we talked about were more down-to-earth, like football and places he'd been. He described Oklahoma City in a way that made me want to see it for myself. One day, he invited me down there for a visit. I could only imagine a trip like that; I certainly couldn't afford one. When he offered to ferry me back and forth in his van, I was torn. He was retired, and I'd earned a few days of vacation. I really hadn't planned to get together with Chuck. However, after some thought, I decided such a trip would probably be OK.

Oklahoma turned out to be far different than I expected. When we got to Oklahoma City, I learned it was one of the biggest cities (in area) in the country. However, it was so spread out that it didn't feel crowded. Chuck and I toured the capitol building, the GM plant, the Cowboy Hall of Fame, and the memorial to the Oklahoma City bombing. Chuck was ten years older than I was, with advanced arthritis, so our explorations of nature were limited to long drives to see the natural wonders of the area. Somehow, nature seemed to be more abundant there. A surprising number of small lakes were scattered everywhere. All kinds of unfamiliar birds flocked and gathered around us wherever we went. Drivers seemed to be more courteous there. People were friendly and relaxed. Down-to-earth and straightforward, they seemed to share my apparently old-fashioned values. I didn't see anything I didn't like about the place.

When Chuck took me home, Tumbleweed seemed to be more insignificant than ever. My job skills had improved to the point where I had been regularly promoted. I was making nine dollars per hour—the most I'd ever made. I was sure it was the most I'd ever make in this hick town. I wanted to do something with my life, but I didn't know what. I sat down again at my decrepit computer to learn about the work world. I tried to get a feel for what jobs were out there. I scrutinized dozens of job descriptions. I learned a lot, but what I found made me feel trapped all over again. The really neat-sounding jobs required college degrees and on-the-job experience. I had a bachelor's degree and an impressive resume. However, if I got a job based on my actual resume, my new employer would expect me to know how to do what they'd hired me to do. For years, I'd been governmental affairs director for a large trade association. I had no idea what I'd done in that job. I couldn't even imagine what kinds of things a governmental affairs director might do.

To get another degree, I'd need a lot of money—more money than I could imagine *ever* earning. Even if I could figure out a way to go to school and hold down a full-time job, it would take more than seven years to earn a degree. Even with a useable degree, I didn't have a lot of time remaining in my life to build the years of experience I'd need to get a decent job, much less establish a career. I finally decided to stop dreaming and limit my search to jobs I realistically might be able to qualify for.

Naturally, I discussed my job search with my two new friends. Both Greg and Chuck were encouraging. Chuck suggested that I look for a job in Oklahoma. Moving that far away from the place I considered home was something I hadn't really thought about. However, I didn't have any ties to anyone in Tumbleweed. In fact, by then, Ken and I had had several frustrating arguments about our relationship. It was starting to look like he'd never agree with my strong feeling that friendship was far more valuable than some kind of romantic attachment. He wouldn't go away, and I was sure we'd never be able to have a relationship we'd both be comfortable with.

Moving to Oklahoma looked more promising by the day. It would be an adventure, and I could put some distance between Ken and me. Shortly after I started focusing my search on jobs in Oklahoma, I was granted an interview with a software development company. The interview must have gone better than I thought it had because, soon after, I was offered a job as a customer service representative for eleven dollars an hour! I never imagined I'd really be able to live anywhere other than Tumbleweed. I quickly packed and moved, impatient to discover more of the world than I had ever imagined I might.

# Fifteen

Prejudice squints when it looks and lies
when it talks.

—*Duchess Abrantes*

Life was rosy for a few months. The Sooner State had a
lot of new things to offer. Chuck taught me how to love
the Sooners. We watched every one of their football games,
and I bought an OU flag for my car. I saw animals and birds
I'd never heard of. Cardinals in Oklahoma were as common
as robins in Colorado. One evening, as I was running, I
almost ran into an armadillo. The weather was capricious
and passionate. From the blazing sun to the enveloping fogs,
glacial ice and nuclear thunderstorms, Mother Nature was a
breathtaking presence that couldn't be ignored.

The apartment I chose was separated by a small strip of
grass and trees from one of the most beautiful biking trails
I'd seen. It encircled a small lake perched slightly above a
major highway. On one side was a splendid view of the city
below. The rest of the trail was protected from the surrounding homes by a strip of trees, ferns, vines, and wildlife.
It felt like a miniature piece of a fairy-tale forest. The wind
was always blowing, so my daily workouts, whether I ran
or rode my bike, were demanding yet refreshing. The wide-
open sky, painted with ever-changing cloud formations,
smiled over everything.

I just knew my new job had real potential. I worked

feverishly to learn everything I could, so I could build this job into a lifelong career. After I'd been there about a month, I started to have computer problems no one else was having. Precisely ninety days after I was hired, I was fired. I was shocked and horrified. When I asked repeatedly for an explanation, my supervisor's answer was, "We are not legally obligated to disclose the reasons for your termination." Every muscle in my body stretched more tightly than I could have imagined. The terror that had found me in Tumbleweed was stronger than ever.

Once again, I was on the street, begging for a job. I finally talked the owner of a landscape maintenance company into putting me to work at seven dollars an hour. Again, I'd have to get at least one second job to pay my basic living expenses. At the end of the summer, no one would need landscape maintenance. I'd have to find another full-time job to replace this one. My faith in my ability to do that was now infinitesimal. My so-called resume included two terminations and a decreasing salary. I still hadn't figured out why I'd been fired, so I didn't have a clue how to fix whatever it was about myself that was so devastatingly defective. Maybe I just didn't "speak Oklahoman."

When I went home, that feeling of isolation intensified. I hadn't considered any factors besides the lake when I chose my apartment. I couldn't know that what started out as an idyllic retreat would end up being the place where I would discover prejudice.

I was one of only a couple of white residents in my apartment complex. Everyone else was black. There had been a single black resident in Tumbleweed, and he was just another member of the community. I couldn't comprehend the nature of prejudice when I left. In my new home, however, I learned quickly. I still believed in spreading sunshine, so I smiled at everyone I met. No one smiled back. The few who even looked at me were apparently repulsed by me or disgusted with something. It wasn't long before I got their message. My way of greeting people I didn't know wasn't working. What else was I doing that was socially unacceptable? My apartment was close to the parking lot, and I could get to the running path from there. I avoided most people, most days.

I started to notice things I hadn't seen before. Many windows had no screens. One of my neighbors knocked on my door and asked if she could use my phone, since hers had been disconnected. Almost everyone had stereos, big-screen TVs, and pets, but the cars in the parking lot were beat up or not working. Trash constantly accumulated throughout the shaded courtyard in the middle of the complex. Every week or so, the custodian relocated the trash into the Dumpster, and it looked the same as the day I first saw it. The next day, clutter sprouted like bindweed. I spent a lot of time at Chuck's house.

One morning, I got angry. I took a trash bag outside. After a few minutes, a young boy on the second floor leaned out of his screenless window and gave me what he seemed to think was a sultry greeting. When I looked up, he smiled softly.

"What're you doin'?" He looked like he was about fourteen years old. I was fifty. *Was he trying to come on to me?*

I answered, "Picking up trash."

"Why?" His smile widened as he winked.

"Because I'm tired of living in a slum," I said.

"Do you want some help?" he asked.

Startled, I answered, "Sure."

"How much you gonna pay me?"

"Nothing!" I couldn't believe it. "You live here, too."

When I reached down again, he disappeared from the window.

The next day at work, I asked my landscaping partner for some kind of explanation.

"You're white," he said. "He's black."

"What does that have to do with anything?" I asked.

"They're still mad at us because we brought them here from Africa and made them slaves."

"I don't own any slaves," I said.

"It doesn't matter," he said. "Slave owners were white. We're white. According to them, we owe 'em."

His explanation made no sense to me. How could someone hate me for something my ancestors might have done decades ago? My first glimpse of prejudice was unsettling. How would I handle it? Prejudice couldn't possibly be one of the Laws of Life...could it?

# Sixteen

My relationship with Chuck was changing. At first, he had given me emotional support and the kind of friendship I'd been looking for. As time went on, however, things changed. His arthritis was getting progressively worse. I started to see how limited his interests were. He loved buffets and football. I didn't like buffets, and we watched so many football games that I started cleaning Chuck's house during the time-outs. Our relationship was starting to look disturbingly familiar. Chuck was starting to act possessive and jealous. My exciting adventure had taken me to the same place I'd left behind.

Throughout this adventure, my other online friend, Greg, and I had kept up our daily emails. I told him everything, including how I felt. I asked for reassurance and advice. He gave me both. I'd started to suspect that sex might be playing a part in Chuck's changing behavior, so Greg and I talked about the potentially destructive nature of that beast. We explored all the possible reasons for my recent termination, from inexperience with office politics to personality to epilepsy. (I'd consistently received good performance reviews, so I didn't believe I was fired for incompetence.) Finally, Greg suggested that I move back home. After all, the closest I'd come to any kind of success was in the state where I'd been born. After some thought, I agreed.

When I told Chuck about my decision, he didn't say anything for a minute. Then he whimpered, "Who's going to take care of me?" I didn't answer; I just looked at him. He was serious! Enraged, I showed him to the door. The next day, I started to feel guilty. After all, friends looked after friends, didn't they? Was I being selfish? What would other people do in my situation? There must be a Law of Life to cover this kind of situation.

While we were pulling weeds the next day, I asked my coworker what he thought.

"He's sixty years old," was his reply. "If he doesn't know how to take care of himself by now…"

I made my decision. I'd move as soon as I found a job.

Greg convinced me that one of the towns along the Colorado Front Range, at the base of the Rocky Mountains, would be the best place to live. I took his word for it. After all, he lived in a tourist town in the foothills; he'd obviously seen more of my home state than I had. Also, he offered to let me stay in his spare bedroom until I found a place of my own.

Immediately, I registered with every online job site I could find. As the summer started to draw to a close, I found a job with a catalog company. I would be taking telephone orders for products advertised in catalogs. I would work from 10 PM until 6:30 AM, so I would earn a few cents more per hour than daytime workers.

Relieved, I started to pack. Greg told me he'd help me move, so I rented a U-Haul. A few days before I was scheduled to pick it up, he called.

"I won't be able to help you after all, Beki," he announced. "I have to go to a meeting."

I felt like I'd been hit with every negative feeling in

the world: panic, abandonment, terror, desperation, anger, and shock. I couldn't believe he'd even promised to help me if he hadn't planned on it! I hadn't made any friends in Oklahoma. Chuck and I were no longer speaking. I couldn't afford to hire a moving company. I couldn't lift my furniture by myself. I had to move out of my apartment. I frantically paced back and forth in my dark living room, trying to think of a solution.

Ken, my friend from Tumbleweed, and I had spoken three or four times since I'd moved here. In desperation, I finally called him and explained my situation. I offered to pay his plane fare if he would come to Oklahoma and help me move. I was convinced he would turn me down. There was no reason for him to take time out of his life to rescue me.

I don't remember the following conversation at all. I only know that I felt like a complete jerk for asking. I do remember Ken was silent for what seemed like an hour before he finally agreed to make the trip. I was relieved.

When I asked him later why he'd come, he said with a wink, "Well, Beki, it was a free airline ticket."

"Seriously," he added, "That's what friends do for each other."

He drove the U-Haul out of the parking lot, and I followed him onto the Interstate. I was full of all kinds of feelings. There was so much about this place I would miss, especially nature at its hot-blooded best. I wouldn't miss my job; I only hoped my next one would be more tolerable. With a lot of luck, I might be able to recognize potential problems and avoid them.

I wouldn't miss Chuck. Evidently, he'd misunderstood all our discussions about friendship. Maybe he saw my move to Oklahoma as proof that I'd changed my mind. I started to consider the possibility that words play an even smaller role in communication than I'd suspected before.

I was looking forward to spending time with Greg. I was starting to think he was the only person in the word who truly understood me.

The trip through the glorious, green wheat fields of Kansas was one of the most beautiful I can remember. I was going home.

# Seventeen

Perfect love is rare indeed—for to be a lover will require that you continually have the subtlety of the very wise, the flexibility of the child, the sensitivity of the artist, the understanding of the philosopher, the acceptance of the saint, the tolerance of the scholar, and the fortitude of the certain.

—*Leo Buscaglia*

By the time I left Oklahoma, I had decided that sex distorted friendship. It wasn't simply a natural expression of friendship after all. Men acted as if sex gave them some kind of ownership rights. They enjoyed nonexclusive affairs, but only with women who were exclusively theirs. I still believed that friendships were infinitely more valuable than exclusive relationships. I was starting to wonder if true friendship with a man was even possible.

Greg and I had discussed the issue repeatedly. We agreed that we wanted the friendship we'd begun on the Internet to last. We hoped that keeping sex out of our relationship would make that possible.

With Greg, I experienced the exhilaration of what I thought was true love—the epitome of friendship. We had everything in common. We endlessly discussed things most people I'd met didn't even think about, like the evolution of a star or the composition of a musical masterpiece. I'd always wanted to experience new things and see the world. He took me to lush Oregon vineyards on a wine-tasting exhibition. We stayed in a beautiful hotel on the beach, where I made my first acquaintance with the Pacific Ocean. He showed me how to find trailheads to breathtaking hikes in Rocky Mountain National Park. He introduced me to the classy sound of jazz, and he took me to indoor and outdoor concerts all along the Front Range. A former piano player in a jazz band, he played his own compositions for me on his magnificent grand piano. Almost every night, we shared a glass of fine wine as we watched the sun set over the mountains from his deck. Our friendship had lasted almost a year. It was the best I'd ever had. My tenuous belief that it might last a lifetime was starting to strengthen.

After a couple of months with Greg, I found an apartment close to work. It was bigger than any apartment I'd rented yet. My bedroom was in a loft, with plenty of room for my computer. With huge windows and a southern exposure, it was very light. Beauregard loved it!

My friendship with Greg didn't change, at least for me. However, one day, just as things with Greg were more perfect than I had imagined possible, he unexpectedly, venomously discarded me. I couldn't believe it.

When I asked why, he told me, "I've been seeing other people, haven't you?"

"What does that have to do with us?" I was confused. From the beginning, we'd agreed that our friendship was nonexclusive. He knew that Ken and I talked on the phone and got together occasionally. I'd always assumed Greg had other women friends he hadn't mentioned.

Greg refused to answer my question. He also refused to budge.

I was devastated. I couldn't even be friends with someone who was my mirror image! His emotional outburst ended our friendship and destroyed my wispy confidence in my ability to make any kind of relationship with any man last. The kind of relationship I wanted was simply not possible. I didn't want to have anything more to do with men.

By then, I'd collected a few people I saw as potential friends. One of them was Karen, my college roommate. I'm not sure why she was still in my life. Maybe I still recognized her because, like my family, we'd kept in touch throughout my experience with seizures. While I was still in Tumbleweed, we'd gotten together once a month. We'd meet for brunch at a dinky café just off the Interstate, a forty-five minute drive for each of us. At first, I'd been anxious, but with each meeting, I felt more and more comfortable. She was easy to be with. We seemed to have a lot in common. We'd both grown up on farms. I felt a kind of bond between us that I hadn't felt with anyone else. Even so, I wasn't sure how to act or what to say to be the person she used to know.

After a while, I discovered I could open my heart to her. Her thoughts on everything, including men, seemed to be grounded in common sense and validated by experience. As we got ready to leave, she always asked, "When do you want to get together next?" That simple question always made me believe that our get-togethers were as fun for her as they were for me. They were certainly different from time spent with men. We talked frequently when I lived in Oklahoma, and we got together periodically after I moved back to Colorado.

I met another potential friend at work. I liked her immediately. She had a great sense of humor and a refreshing forthrightness. Like Greg, she loved thinking and talking about a universe of ideas and a world full of history and diversity. Every time I needed a shot of intellectual stimulation, we'd have breakfast, spiced with ideas and laughs.

She was ten years older than I was; eventually she became a confidante and advisor.

Then there was Ken. Even though we still had very little in common, I'd started to accept him as an important part of my life. He was very down-to-earth; theory and possibilities bored him. Why things happened was far less important to him than how they worked. He'd taken regular fishing trips to the mountains, but he'd spent most of his life in Tumbleweed. He hadn't thought much about more exciting adventures.

After he helped me move, he called me regularly. We got together frequently. We didn't talk about "our" future; we focused on what was happening right now. I was still trying to identify the Laws of Life. It seemed like whenever he called, I was trying to decide how to deal with some kind of unexpected issue. He would listen patiently, answer my questions, and give me advice and support. He seemed to think my behavior was mostly appropriate. I didn't always agree, but his assurances were comforting.

One evening, he said, "Beki, come here! Look at this sunset!" As we absorbed the magnificent colors, I realized that life had lost a lot of its original sparkle for me. I hadn't even noticed night's approach for a while. I'd stopped looking around when I ran. Suddenly, I wanted to recover some of the excitement I used to feel about the world.

One day, I heard about Trail Ridge Road. At 12,183 feet above sea level, it was the highest paved road in the United States. My dad told me I'd been there, but I didn't remember the trip. I asked Ken if he'd ever negotiated that road. When he said he hadn't, I suggested that we do some exploring, starting there. Camping trips wouldn't cost much, and we could plan our trips around holidays. We combined our money and bought a tent. We dragged our sleeping bags out of our closets and took off.

We met people from all over the world at places that

were within driving distance for us. We crossed the Continental Divide on roads that were so narrow they made your hair stand on end. We saw parks full of dinosaur bones, remains of long-dormant volcanoes, ancient cliff dwellings, and hidden sand dunes. We stood on canyon rims, dams, and bridges. We watched mountain goats walk nonchalantly along seemingly perpendicular mountainsides. We soaked in natural hot springs. We rode on narrow gauge railroads and gondolas. The trips were exciting, colorful, informative, and fun. They gave me a chance to forget about the real world for a few days. Most importantly, they injected me with a good dose of life's much-missed sparkle.

After Greg's vitriolic dumping, men became more of a problem. I didn't want to date anyone, but when some man learned I was unattached, he wouldn't leave me alone. I didn't want to be rude, so I answered their questions as I tried to refuse their invitations.

When I mentioned my problem to Ken, he suggested I use him as an excuse. At first, I wouldn't even consider the idea. I still didn't want to have any kind of exclusive relationship. I especially didn't want to give Ken any reason to think I was more serious about him than I was. Finally, however, I'd had my fill of exasperating phone calls. I agreed to an exclusive relationship with Ken, as long as there were no commitments. We would have fun together until it stopped being fun. I would use our relationship as a "male repellant" to simplify my life. At first, I saw that decision as a kind of weakness, just one more example of my ignorance of people. After a while, however, it proved to be a very effective way to politely keep men at a distance.

My ideas about friendship hadn't changed. I still looked at it as the most valuable relationship people could share. I was starting to meet people with common interests and outlooks. I was learning that sharing my life with friends and family was indeed a most beautiful way to spend it.

# Eighteen

There are, in every age, new errors to be rectified and new prejudices to be opposed.

—*Samuel Johnson*

My new job wasn't hard. Shortly after I walked through the doors of the shiny new building and settled into my cubicle, I was directed to a small meeting room for a brief, enthusiastic orientation. My supervisor was a short, pudgy redhead with a permanently sour expression, who turned out to be more domineering, demanding, and demeaning than anyone I'd worked for yet. Fortunately, I didn't have a lot of contact with her since I came to work as she was leaving. I hoped I could avoid trouble by doing a good job and staying out of sight.

I also hoped this job would be temporary. There was very little chance for advancement, and the pay was excruciatingly low. Once again, I would need at least one second job to feel even the tiniest bit secure. I used my time off during the day to look for additional work. Job hunting was starting to seem like the only stable work I'd ever have. I scoured the classified ads every day, just as I had in Tumbleweed. The Utopia I'd been counting on when I left Oklahoma was nowhere to be seen. Colorado's technology boom had crashed, and hundreds of educated, skilled, experienced workers were unemployed. Employers who weren't in the middle of layoffs didn't even have to acknowledge resumes of people who needed training. Qualifications for the most basic job included at least a bachelor's degree. It would take a lot of hard work and even more luck to find a job with any career potential.

I never suspected that prejudice would play any kind of role in my job search. The idea that my age or gender could instantly remove me from candidate pools never even crossed my mind. From my perspective, female coworkers my age seemed to be more dedicated and conscientious than men of any age.

One day, an ad appeared for a general worker in a paint store. It wasn't an administrative position. It would require some physical labor. It sounded like it might be fun. I spruced up and drove over to the small shop. When I walked through the door, an arrogant young man with blond, spiked hair was stocking a shelf. He was clearly irritated at my interruption.

"I'm here about the ad in the—"

He looked at me in disbelief, shook his head, and kept lifting paint cans. "The position's been filled."

"The ad just came out this morning," I said.

"The position's been filled," he repeated. His attitude was clearly: *Get a life, you old broad.*

I didn't believe him, but what could I say?

I didn't consider epilepsy to be any kind of an issue for employers, either. Years ago, in Tumbleweed, I had met a relative whose son had epilepsy. One day, she asked me if I'd like to meet him and watch a video of one of his grand mal seizures. My first reaction was an enthusiastic "Yes!" It would probably be the only chance I'd have to see what a seizure was actually like. When I told Ken about my upcoming trip, however, he asked somberly, "Do you think that's a good idea?" As we talked, I started to get the impression that witnessing a seizure was the last thing

I should do. By the time I actually sat down in front of the TV, I was convinced I was about to see some kind of horrific event. Instead, to my relief, the video was very interesting. It simply showed how a "brainstorm" affected a body. Afterward, I spent a few hours with this very normal family. For me, the visit had been like a scientific field trip. I couldn't understand how seizures could intimidate anyone.

Since then, I've learned that very few people seem to see seizures as merely interesting biological events. Most people, including doctors, don't seem to know much about epilepsy at all. Even those who are aware of its existence apparently misunderstand it. They seem to think seizures are life threatening, and that people who have them should be avoided at all costs.

I hadn't learned a lot about life yet. It didn't occur to me that anyone would reject my job application because they were afraid I might have a thirty-second brain malfunction one of these days. After all, my resume was packed with other valid reasons for rejection. As a result, I addressed what I assumed were the legitimate issues: lack of experience and education, and a less-than-ideal job history. I spotlighted my proven ability to quickly learn whatever I'd needed to know for each job. I emphasized my reliability: I'd never missed an hour of work, even though I'd usually held down more than one job at a time.

I couldn't remember what my life had been like when I was having seizures. I didn't know that many people with seizures have problems with mood swings or other erratic behavior. That part of my history didn't have anything to do with me now. My seizures had been completely controlled for years; there was no reason to expect any more in the future. To me, epilepsy was just one explanation for my memory loss, and that loss was the primary reason for my fall from the heights of success to my current situation.

Besides, choosing not to hire someone with epilepsy was illegal. I assumed most employers followed the law.

For most people with epilepsy, living with unwarranted discrimination—prejudice—is a fact of life. For me, living with warranted discrimination was an additional reality. I could empathize with a business owner whose livelihood depended on his employees. It had to be hard to justify taking a chance on someone without an education or a proven record of success. Hiring a unmarried, middle-aged woman with a cockeyed story about no memory would be even riskier. The only employers who seriously considered my application were those with high turnover, or who paid so little they didn't have much to lose.

I felt like I was trying to race through quicksand. The harder I struggled, the faster I sank. The only way I could see to fight discrimination was to discover the Laws of Life. No one would take me seriously until I knew how to behave appropriately. They were hidden more deeply than I had imagined, but I had to find those laws.

# Nineteen

I hadn't given any thought to the neighborhood when I
signed the lease for my apartment. Soon after I moved
in, I started to see that it was a bad one. My neighbors constantly played music as loudly as they could. One of them
had a barking dog he refused to control. It was barking when
I got home from work in the morning, and it didn't stop all
day. For months, I fought unsuccessfully with its owner so
I could get some sleep.

At last, my college roommate Karen encouraged me to
buy my own place. She convinced me that real estate was
the best investment I could make. Trembling, I emptied my
savings account and became a homeowner.

The eight-hundred-square-foot, one-bedroom, one-bath
condominium was a move up for me. It had an open design
with big windows and a southern exposure. I didn't need air
conditioning; the capricious breeze could waft between the
windows. The surrounding, mature trees cooled and protected the condo. A second-story unit, it felt more secure
than a place on the ground floor. It cost more than what
I'd wanted to spend, but the Realtor convinced me that

payments of more than half my income were well within established investment guidelines.

That purchase was the biggest mistake I ever made. As soon as I moved in, I discovered the seller had lied to me about major repair issues. When I asked why maintenance on the common grounds wasn't being done, all I got were shrugs. The owners of the seven other condos in the building routinely refused to consider repairs to the buckling, sinking sidewalks and landings, the disintegrating parking lot, or the sickly landscape. It was inconceivable. How could people be so resolutely lethargic about preserving what was probably the biggest investment of their lives?

Regular homeowners' association (HOA) meetings were never held. The rare, special meeting consisted of a potluck with homemade beer and a discussion of parking problems. Recordkeeping of any kind was practically non-existent. The directors of the HOA were handling eight owners' dues money, but they seemed profoundly insulted that anyone would even suggest they keep track of it. The treasurer never prepared financial statements, and she refused to provide me with any kind of financial information. No one else in the building seemed to care about what happened to their dues.

My dad finally paid a lawyer to write several letters asking board members to follow the bylaws. After seven months, I was finally given a balance sheet with "Financial Statement" printed proudly at the top of the page. Our monthly expenses were lower than our dues income, but our checking account was precariously close to empty. Either all the dues weren't being collected or money was being spent that wasn't included on the statement. No one could explain any of the discrepancies. The HOA president finally admitted that some expenses were handled with a kind of trade agreement. For example, he purchased an extension ladder that everyone was free to use (but was nowhere to be seen), so he was excused from his dues payment the month he bought that invisible asset. There were no receipts for the purchase.

I'm sure my attitude didn't help. I couldn't understand the benefit of being "fluffy," especially when the issue was money. Every question I asked seemed to send the board members further into their black hole of secret spending. All I could do was helplessly watch my property deteriorate—and my hard-earned cash vaporize. I was learning that less than half of my take-home pay was not enough to cover all my living expenses.

After a year, I decided to sell the place. It's been on the market ever since. The last Realtor who listed it refused to renew my contract when she couldn't lure a single person through the door. I tried to understand why no one even wanted to look at it. One agent told me the property had a negative curb appeal. Also, the pool of potential buyers for my tiny second-floor cubbyhole was depressingly insignificant. Young, single people or childless couples who would have no problem negotiating the stairs were the only real possibilities I could see.

The neighborhood was most certainly another factor. It was an older part of town, made up of primarily rentals. Most of our neighbors had beat-up cars and trucks squeezed into every available inch of curb. Adjoining lawns were mowed sporadically, and scattered trash was a permanent part of the surrounding landscape. Lately, signs of gang activity had started to appear.

The market didn't help, either. Residential construction had exploded all along the Front Range. Single-family homes were being sold with all kinds of enticements, so first-time homeowners didn't have to start small. As a result, the condominium market was flat. I paid $325 for a professional appraiser to tell me my "mobile home without wheels" was worth $22,000 less than what I'd paid for it three years before. I bought a "For Sale by Owner" sign for the front lawn. I didn't include a price; I would sell it to the person with the best offer. The one person who came to see the place disappeared silently, without a trace. Slowly and unwillingly, I accepted the fact that I might be stuck with my "investment."

My relationship with the HOA's board of directors deteriorated faster than the property. No matter what I tried, there was only one other homeowner who seemed to care about maintenance at all. I couldn't convince any of the rest of them to even try to care. After a while, I volunteered to handle the HOA's money so I could stem the tide of vanishing dollars. I also started taking care of the landscape so we could stop paying landscape maintenance "professionals" we rarely saw.

Again, ignorance had raised its ugly head. It had created another overwhelming obstacle in my life. Trying to live within my means was as hard as it had ever been, and my financial future didn't look promising. My "investment" had cost me more than I'd ever be able to recover. Jean de la Fontaine once said, "A person often meets his destiny on the road he took to avoid it." Maybe my destiny was to learn how to live with nothing.

# Twenty

During the years following my last seizure, I'd found
several low-paying part-time or temporary jobs to
supplement my full-time income. I'd made cold phone calls
to set appointments for an insurance agent. I'd worked as
a receptionist for H&R Block. I'd mowed lawns and pulled
weeds in the summer. I'd shoveled sidewalks and driveways
the few times it snowed in the dry winters.

Every time I deposited my paycheck, I was thankful I
still had a full-time job. However, the high turnover at the
catalog company constantly reminded me of the fragility
of employment. As a result, I spent every spare minute job
hunting. I found several more part-time jobs. I worked as an
office manager with an established appraiser; I found a few
houses to clean; I worked as a counselor for developmen-
tally disabled people; and I helped maintain the landscape
for a ritzy housing development.

The job with the appraiser looked so promising that I
quit my full-time job at the catalog company, as well as the
part-time counseling job. My new boss, Clyde, promised
me a raise at the end of landscaping season, so I could afford
to take some appraisal classes. He also assured me he'd train
me to do his field work. In no time, I'd be qualified to start

making my own appraisals. I was sure I was starting down the path to a stable career.

While I waited for the promised hands-on experience, I organized his office. I learned how to use his financial software. I upgraded his accounting system. I called customers with past-due balances and eventually collected over forty-two thousand dollars. After four months, it became clear he was dragging his feet. I would have to ask for the past-due raise and training he'd promised.

I prepared spreadsheets to demonstrate that my collections alone justified a healthy raise. In addition, since I'd started mailing monthly statements, payments were regularly pouring into his checking account. As soon as he trained me to work in the field, I could increase the number of appraisals we could complete, as well as his profits.

When everything was ready, I gathered up my flimsy courage and asked Clyde for a meeting. I was sure the only thing he might want to negotiate would be the amount of the raise. Instead, he flatly stated, "Any raise would jeopardize my business." He said nothing about any training. When I reminded him of the promises he'd made when he hired me, he shook his head. "Any raise would jeopardize my business." When I showed him all my spreadsheets, he was unimpressed.

I left the office dumbfounded. Based on my past experience, I was sure that if I pushed the issue, I'd be fired.

Once again, I'd fallen for an employer's vacant promises. The end of landscaping season was fast approaching. My income from this job and my other part-time jobs wouldn't cover my fixed monthly expenses. I'd have to find some way to make more money. Finding another traditional job before the end of the landscaping season would be impossible at best. Increasing the number of cleaning customers was my only hope. My boss assured me that time spent marketing my cleaning business wouldn't be a problem. My hours were flexible; I just had to make sure I worked five hours each day in his office.

I joined a group of local small business owners who met weekly for lunch and networking. The adjustment to my weekly schedule to accommodate the lunches was barely noticeable. However, when he saw it, Clyde blew up. I assured him I'd still be working the agreed-upon five hours each day. He informed me that if I continued to go to the meetings, I'd have to resign.

I scrutinized his face. He was serious! After an uncomfortable silence, I agreed to leave, on the condition that he sign a termination letter to qualify me for unemployment compensation. He didn't say anything. I wrote the letter, put it on his desk, sat down, and waited. When it was clear I wasn't going to leave without his signature, he reluctantly scribbled his name.

I had agreed to stay on for two weeks to train my replacement. A week after she arrived, I learned what he was paying her. I stormed into his office. "You're paying her a dollar an hour more than what you paid me? Won't that 'jeopardize your business'?"

He didn't answer. I went back to my desk, wrote out my final check, placed it on his desk and demanded his signature. He refused to sign it.

"You'd better check the federal employment laws," I said angrily. "You are required to pay every employee for every minute they work."

He didn't move.

I moved closer to his desk and pronounced, "You are a bully, a liar, and a cheat!" emphasizing each word with a finger pointed at his chest. He stood up, went to the phone, and pressed 9-1-.

"Check the federal employment laws," I repeated, as I turned to go. "You aren't through with me until I get my money."

When I started my car, Mariah Carey's version of the song "Hero" had just started. I listened to the familiar words and started to cry. After six years of banging my head against the boulders of the work world, reality finally started to seep through the cracks in my thick skull and into my tangled brain. My dreams of success were just droplets in the mist above a waterfall: breathtaking and doomed. Whenever I started to drown, a job appeared, like a reassuring sandbar in the middle of the stream. People basking in job security would answer my call for help and start to pull me toward them. Then, just as I started to feel a little of stability's sunshine, they'd let go with a laugh and roll over.

Again and again, I'd convinced people to pay for the privilege of teaching me to perform some unrecognizable function. I'd mastered the tasks, then lost the jobs. My instincts were apparently nonexistent, counterproductive, or downright destructive. My logic seemed to be equally flawed. The information I'd devoured apparently hadn't given me knowledge or adaptability. My perceptions of the working world seemed to be skewed just enough to make it impossible for me to fit in, and I didn't have enough experience even to make educated guesses.

I still believed everything that happened had to contain at least one clue to at least one Law of Life. However, after my endless scrutiny of each encounter, I'd been remarkably unable to glimpse even one of those laws. I didn't want to keep repeating the devastating experiences, but I had to consider the possibility that I might just be hopelessly ignorant.

As the song ended with the words "A hero lies in you," I shook my head. So far, all I'd done was heroically fail. I started my car and drove home. I never wanted to give up as badly as I did at that moment.

# Twenty-one

By the time I got home, I knew giving up wasn't possible. The only thing of value I possessed was an unblemished credit rating. If I ran away from my mortgage, I'd lose that rating. If I stopped applying for jobs, I'd lose my unemployment benefits. Thanks to my other part-time jobs, I wasn't completely unemployed. I wouldn't receive full benefits, but I needed every bit of income I could come up with to keep milk in my refrigerator.

I attended classes at the local unemployment office to learn how to write effective resumes. I applied for every job I might even remotely qualify for. Sometimes I sent resumes that included only my recent experience. Other times, I listed my college degree and all my forgotten accomplishments. Sometimes I included a cover letter, referencing a "brain injury resulting in extensive memory loss." I tried different formats, colored ink, colored paper, oversized envelopes. I made dozens of phone calls. I called on people who were hiring and people who weren't. I contacted different people in the same company or bugged the same person repeatedly. Each time, when I told my story to the person who granted me a rare interview, I was met with blank stares and pointed to the door.

Not all the dismissals were polite. A fellow member of my business networking lunch group had referred me to the head of a network marketing company that provided ongoing legal services. After I mentioned my memory loss, he put his feet up on his desk, clasped his hands behind his head, and said, "Well, *that* must be convenient!" I didn't know what to say. Of all the words I could think of to describe my experience, "convenient" had never been anywhere on the list. *What could possibly be convenient about losing my past?*

As I walked out of his office, I realized with a jolt that the guy simply hadn't believed me. *Why would anyone fabricate such a ridiculous story?* I considered the question for hours. The only kind of person who might even think of trying to erase their past might be a convicted felon. I was pretty sure I didn't have any kind of criminal record. At some point, I realized he probably wasn't the only person who hadn't believed me. Maybe my situation was simply incomprehensible. Then again, there were plenty of people out there with implausible stories. I'd just met a snow-blind UPS driver. He didn't say much about his condition. The only effect it had on his job was a temporary route change during snowstorms. I wondered if anyone had accused him of faking it. I guessed it didn't really matter. There was no way to prove that I had no retrograde memory. If people didn't believe me, there wasn't much I could do about it.

People kept telling me, "Hang in there. You live in America, the land of opportunity. You can do anything you truly want to do." I agreed with them. Society didn't. I was a fifty-three-year-old woman with a worthless bachelor's degree and six years of life experience. I didn't have a lot to offer an employer. My resume was a tattered quilt of mindless, marginal, dead-end jobs that had given me some primitive, limited experience. Each addition to that willy-nilly collection of jobs seemed to be doing its part to ensure an even more precarious future.

I had an uncommon health issue that many seemed to view as a scary disability. I didn't understand their reactions or how to handle them. My memory loss seemed to be equally hard to comprehend or believe.

I was naïve. I was intense—maybe too intense to get along with. Maybe my lack of a past made it hard to establish rapport. I believed in an honest day's work for a day's pay, in a world where many people seemed to take pride in finding creative ways to slack off. I consistently avoided coworkers I didn't respect, in a world where the ability to brownnose was starting to seem more valuable than competence and hard work. Maybe my aversion to office politics was lethal.

I couldn't change my situation. The only thing I could change was the way I coped with it. One of my favorite sayings was, "If you always do what you've always done, you'll always get what you've always gotten." Years ago, the neurophysiologist had told me I had a tendency to try the same things repeatedly, even when they didn't work. My life to date seemed to prove that statement. I'd repeatedly tried to make a living working for someone else. That hadn't worked. Somehow, I'd have to find something I hadn't tried before. I didn't see myself as particularly creative, but I had to think of something. I racked my brain for direction. My survival would depend on my ability to fill a need within society in some other way.

# Twenty-two

My sister Lindsay had owned her own business for over
a decade. A firm believer in self-employment, she recommended I design a business around skills I already had.
I had a good basic knowledge of computer systems and
hardware. I was familiar with several software programs,
from word processing to financial spreadsheets and accounting packages. I'd consistently received excellent evaluations
for my customer service skills. I could successfully sell
things on the phone and in person. I'd prepared tax returns
for my HOA, as well as itemized returns for myself. I knew
how to clean, pull weeds, prune trees, and mow lawns. I
had a lot of stamina. I enjoyed working.

I didn't have any extra money for startup expenses, so
I couldn't buy a building, rent an office, or purchase inven-
tory. The business I chose would have to be a service I
could provide from home. Lindsay suggested all kinds of
possible endeavors. We first explored interesting enter-
prises with growth potential. Maybe I could help people
organize their businesses. Maybe I could introduce new
computer owners to the Internet, or demonstrate features
of their factory-installed software. Maybe I could design
accounting systems for small business owners. Every option

we considered would be personalized to fit each customer's unique needs.

I was sure I could quickly learn whatever was necessary to make each enterprise successful. I wasn't so sure I could sell myself to potential customers. After all, I'd been able to convince only a few people to hire me over the years. My people skills didn't seem to be that great, either. None of my skimpy experience precisely fit any of the businesses we were considering. Why should anyone agree to pay me for services I hadn't actually performed in the past? How could I keep customers if I didn't know enough to predict the inevitable, mostly unknown issues that were sure to appear?

There were two services I believed I could sell. I could honestly say I'd been cleaning and maintaining landscapes professionally, albeit part-time, for over four years. Both would be simple businesses. I couldn't imagine many problems I couldn't handle that might crop up with either. I'd be working mostly alone, so I wouldn't need exceptional people skills.

There were a couple of disadvantages to both potential businesses. From the moment I'd scraped the gray out of my first apartment, I'd detested cleaning. It was mind-numbing, hard labor. Landscaping was more enjoyable, but it was seasonal.

I finally decided that year-round cleaning with summer landscape maintenance would be easiest for me to sell. I could build on my current customer base until I could live solely on income from my business. The possibility that I might have to clean houses until I died was repulsive. No matter, my choice was clear: clean houses or practice living on the street.

From the minute I sat down at my computer to design my business, the phone lines between my living room and my sister's home were smoking. I was in a constant state of panic. I needed advice on marketing. I had to anticipate and answer customers' questions. I had to familiarize myself with government regulations and tax laws. Lindsay was the only person I knew with in-depth knowledge of everything required to run a business. I felt guilty taking so much of her time, but she always assured me my calls weren't a problem.

My dad recommended calling his sister, a former manager for a national cleaning franchise. Her advice was unequivocal: "You tell them what you will do—and what you *won't* do—in no uncertain terms. If you don't, they'll take advantage of you." I couldn't imagine how or why people would take advantage of a cleaning lady, but it made sense to establish a clear understanding of the specific job I would do for each customer. I developed a form with a list of all kinds of standard tasks, as well as blanks for customers' special requests. I scheduled an initial meeting before we agreed to a regular cleaning schedule. We prioritized the things I'd be doing and discussed how much time the customer wanted me to spend. We agreed that I would complete as many tasks as I could in the time allotted. When I finished, I would check off all completed items and leave the list for their review. Whenever a customer wanted me to do something special, we would specify which task or tasks would be skipped that time. I charged by the hour, just in case my aunt was right.

Marketing my business wasn't fun. I advertised briefly in the local paper. I printed hundreds of flyers. Ken and I scattered them all over prosperous-looking neighborhoods. I took them into doctor's offices, health clubs, grocery stores, senior centers, and recreation centers. I asked small business owners if they needed someone to clean their offices. I offered discounts to current customers for referrals, as well as to new customers. The leads group I'd joined had started producing referrals, so I visited other networking groups in town.

One by one, people gave me a chance to prove I was worth their business. My education and experience were rarely questioned. If I did a good job, they asked me to clean on a regular basis. They didn't care who I used to be; all they cared about was the quality of my work. Most of my customers had jobs, so I didn't have a lot of contact with them. Some were there when I cleaned, and we became friends. However, I never felt entirely comfortable with any of them. I still doubted my ability to maintain lasting friendships. Besides, our professional relationship was always my top priority. As a result, I never felt free to be completely open with any of them about anything.

When I wasn't cleaning, I was learning how to be a better cleaner. I read everything I could find about the methods, supplies, and products professionals used. I converted a gym bag into an efficient "tools of the trade transporter." Colorado State University's Extension service offered a Master Gardener course that helped me expand the landscaping services I provided in the summer.

After about a year, when I plopped my bag of cleaning supplies on the floor one day, I became aware of a strange feeling. I couldn't identify it at first. It felt like I'd taken a deep breath. I had to think about it for a few minutes. Finally, I realized I was no longer terrified. I was starting to earn enough money to pay the bills. More importantly, my survival didn't depend on just one person anymore. If I lost a customer or two, I'd still have enough money to make ends meet.

Even though I felt more secure than I ever had, I didn't celebrate, or cheer, or even smile. I wasn't going to take anything for granted. I vowed to keep working as hard as ever.

# Twenty-three

All that we know is, nothing can be known.

—*Karl Kraus*

One night, I was putting my cleaning rags into the washing machine when it hit me. There were no Laws of Life! There really were no unwritten, intrinsic guidelines to appropriate behavior that everyone unthinkingly followed. If there were, there would be no need for laws, ordinances, treaties, or religious leaders to define appropriate behavior within a community or nation. There would be no need for legislatures or city councils to hammer out guidelines for acceptable behaviors within their jurisdictions. There would be no need for police forces, judges, jails, or armies to enforce laws or ordinances.

The realization was unexpected, and my reaction to it surprised me. I would have anticipated feeling more emotion, even devastation, but all I felt was recognition. Maybe I'd suspected the truth for a while, and it took some final domino of experience to topple what I now recognized as an obsession. It was unsettling to admit that the conviction I'd used to interpret my every experience for the last several years was an invalid hypothesis. Even so, in some ways, it was a relief. I could now appreciate that different reactions might be appropriate with different people in the same situation. I no longer had to try to fit my every move into some elusive, cookie-cutter mold.

I thought for a minute. Life's challenges would be different from now on. I'd have to identify my own laws of life. Appropriate behavior would still depend on the situation, but I'd also have to consider the people in each situation. In every reaction, I'd have to listen closely to them to understand the reasons behind their actions. I'd have to recognize their values, their unique laws of life. I'd have to learn how to live by my laws while adapting to theirs.

I was now cautiously optimistic about my ability to deal successfully with people on a casual or temporary basis. Long-term personal or professional relationships, however, were still daunting. I'd come a long way, but I still hadn't accepted the possibility that a relationship could survive even one mistake. I was still convinced that the only person who made mistakes in relationships was me, since everyone else undoubtedly knew the score. Disagreeing with others' perceptions of what had happened was more than just a waste of time. It could also affect relationships—especially in the work world, where potential employers talk to ex-bosses.

I went out on my deck and sat down in my two-dollar plastic lawn chair. I wasn't sure how to feel about this revelation. Everything was so clear now. Where had this obsession come from? Why had it taken so long to see the truth? I was sure there must be some psychological explanation for it. I supposed nothing would really change except the way I spent my "thinking time." I knew I had a lot of work to do to make up for the time I'd wasted searching for a nonexistent Truth.

# Twenty-four

It's not what you know, it's who you
know.

—*Unknown*

When I moved back to Colorado, my dad had recently
retired from his position as the chief of staff to one
of the two Colorado senators. Shortly after his retirement,
he was asked to be a member of a commission made up
of representatives from three states. A federal agency had
directed Colorado, Wyoming, and Nebraska to come up
with a way to deliver enough water to the Platte River to
ensure the survival of three endangered species. Water law
is complicated, and people who understand it are rare. The
agency wanted to take advantage of Dad's lifelong experience as a legislator and agricultural water user. He was one
of the few people in the state who had an in-depth understanding of the unique way Colorado managed its limited
supply of water.

One day, as I listened, fascinated, to his review of the
latest meeting, I said I'd love to work somewhere in Colorado's "water world." He thought a minute.

"Why don't you talk to old Luke?" he finally suggested.
A fellow commissioner, Luke headed one of our thirsty
state's highly respected water conservancy districts.

After several phone calls, Luke agreed to see me. I
explained my situation and asked for a job. I was willing to

do anything. I would work full-time or part-time whenever they needed help. Maybe I could eventually work my way into a rewarding career where I could make a difference.

To my amazement, he hired me. I worked half a day a week, and was on call for the rest of the week. I answered phones, copied information packets, helped set up meeting rooms, and did anything else I was asked to do. In the meantime, I got to know everyone in the district and asked questions nonstop. From the first moment I walked through the door, I kept my eyes open for other opportunities in Colorado's world of water. I checked every internal job opening that came up and learned about other water-related jobs throughout the state.

At one point, I was told that water commissioner jobs in Colorado required no experience or education. I learned everything I could about a water commissioner's duties, from measuring water flow to recording procedures. After our initial discussion, the division engineer told me to call him once a month to see if there were any openings. Within a year, I was offered an entry-level position in a small town close to Colorado's eastern border.

This was the opportunity I'd dreamed of! I started to make plans for the move. Just as I was lining up a Realtor to sell my condo, I decided I should tell my future supervisor about my memory loss. Shortly after that, he called to tell me I wasn't qualified for the job after all. They apologized for not telling me the job required a degree in hydrology, as well as seven years of related experience. Devastated, I wondered what would have happened if I hadn't mentioned my memory loss. Until that moment, I had been categorically opposed to lying. I started to wonder if complete honesty might not always be productive.

My first year at the district was nerve-racking. Most tasks I was given were quite detailed. Each week, I learned something new. Often, by the time I was asked to repeat a task, weeks, or even months, had passed and I had to ask for instructions again. Every time that happened, I felt more incompetent. To complicate things further, my cleaning business kept growing. I could no longer be at the district's beck and call. Another person was hired, and I was no longer asked to work more than the four scheduled hours per week. I saw my chance for full-time work evaporate. Pretty soon, I was coming to work, doing very little, and waiting for the axe to fall.

I wasn't feeling much more secure about my cleaning business. I was in the best physical shape I could remember, but I didn't know how long my aging body would bear up under the constant abuse. More importantly, I'd come to realize that a cleaning business is quite mercurial. One-time cleanings were welcome additions to my bank account, but they were also completely unpredictable. My regular customers paid me to be dependable, but they didn't think twice about canceling their scheduled time. Maybe they were going out of town for a couple of weeks. Maybe money was tight that month. If I didn't want to lose their business, I had to hold their time slot open. As a result, I didn't have enough customers to justify hiring any employees, but I didn't have enough available hours in the day to increase my customer base or, consequently, my income.

Colorado's high unemployment rate didn't help. The papers were full of articles about layoffs and business closings. As a result, there was always someone promising better service at lower prices. Illegal aliens were a very real threat. I couldn't afford to lose customers, but if I lowered my prices, I wouldn't have enough income to support myself. Marketing was a constant effort. I hated sales more than cleaning. It took tons of flyers, advertising, personal referrals, and time to gain even a few customers. My work load left no time for developing other skills. Once again, I was starting to feel trapped.

One day, the district's human resources director called me into her office. I steeled myself. *Here it comes!* To my surprise, she didn't fire me. She told me they were hiring another custodian. "Would you be interested in applying for the position?"

Her question startled me. I didn't think employers ever approached people about job openings. The interview went well. They offered me the job. I asked for time to consider everything.

On the downside, I'd once again be dependent on a single employer. My future would still depend on my aging body, rather than my mind, and the wages were lower than what I'd been making. Also, I still hadn't uncovered more than a conglomeration of guesses about why I'd been fired from my previous jobs. There was no reason to believe I was any more capable of avoiding termination than I had ever been.

On the other hand, I'd heard that jobs in government were more secure than those in private enterprise. In this case, working in a water district would undoubtedly be more secure than housecleaning. (People can live with dust on their furniture; no one can live without water.) Competition for my job wouldn't include people working in the underground cash economy. The work would be easier on my body since I'd be working only forty hours a week and I'd be using better equipment. My daily drive time would decrease from hours to minutes. My overall earnings, including the benefit package, would be close to my current income. I'd get regular raises, paid vacations, and an employer-paid retirement account. Most importantly, I would have a steady income. The security I'd been looking for forever was at my fingertips. I decided to accept their offer.

The district turned out to be a great place to work, and I still enjoy it today. My work ethic and philosophy fit perfectly. I work mostly alone, so my chances of screwing up are minimal. The hours are ideal: I work mostly at night, so I can spend my mornings looking for work I truly love to supplement my wages and ensure my future well-being.

# Twenty-five

People frequently tell me that I've overcome a lot of adversity. I'm sure they're trying to compliment me, but their words don't feel like they apply to me. They bring to mind some superhero, holding his sword aloft, smiling through clenched teeth and slapping mountains aside as he charges headlong toward a goal. I've had a goal, all right—survival—but the path to that goal has been hidden and full of detours. I've rarely felt confident, much less invincible. Besides, it seems like I've gotten myself into as many pickles as I've gotten myself out of. I've lived through a lot, but I'm not sure I've overcome much.

People also tell me that most people would have given up a long time ago. Giving up, however, has never been an option. The only way we can give up is to choose to die. Very few people make that choice, and countless live through far more adversity than I. Like most people I know, I did whatever I could to solve the problems that came my way. Each attempt made sense to me. Some of them worked. Some of them didn't.

Life isn't always easy. In fact, a lot of times, it can be downright harsh. Chalk it up to luck or weather or poor health or race or gender or locality or economic hardship, it really doesn't matter. Crises will march into our lives like Huns bent on destruction. The way we deal with them will determine our quality of life and, in some cases, our very survival. Our every reaction can show us something about ourselves. How we choose to use our knowledge will determine our destinies and create our futures. How we choose to interpret the events of our lives will determine our levels of satisfaction with our journeys.

Each of us is faced with very real barriers throughout our lives, many of which we're unable to impact. Most of us can't affect the global economy, a soft real estate market, or a corporate downsizing. We can't change our age, our height, or our inherited traits. In my case, my options have also been severely limited by society's perceptions of epilepsy and memory loss; and these are things I can do little about. I'll never be an educated man with a lifetime of experiences to offer an employer. I'm a fifty-six-year-old female novice whose life began at age forty-seven.

It's hard to know what to do with the challenges we *can* impact. In my case, many of the predicaments I found myself in were the products of ignorance and naïveté. After all, when you don't know what kinds of trouble you can get yourself into, you can easily make ridiculous choices.

For example, because I knew I was ignorant, I always felt vulnerable around people. I knew I couldn't avoid them; they were involved in my life no matter how independent I tried to be. I worked for people. I ran into people everywhere I went. Even when I tried to be a hermit, I was forced to deal with people to handle the everyday details of life. I did what I could to appear to belong in their world.

Also, because I was naïve, I believed that everyone else's piles of experiences made them somehow wiser than me. I trusted everyone but myself. As a result, I learned that some people would take advantage of my ignorance. I learned that recommendations from people who had never been in my shoes often would not work for me. In a broader sense, I learned that, in the amazing complexity of life, what worked for one person could destroy someone else. Those lessons, along with all the other lessons I learned over the last nine years, cost me self-confidence, money, and time. They also made me stronger and, hopefully, wiser. It's possible that I even learned things I didn't need to know in my past.

I appreciate my ignorance in many ways. It hid my limitations and encouraged me to explore and grow. When anything is possible, everything is an adventure. Discovery, from the beauty of nature to the intricacies of love, is breathtaking. Thanks to my ignorance, it's possible I've traveled to places I may never have gone if I'd remembered my first forty-seven years.

People still intimidate me, but now I know that, no matter how intelligent I am, I can't absorb the collective wisdom people have acquired over the ages without help. I can't comprehend all the subtleties of our civilization all by myself. I can't single-handedly protect myself from all the rocks and rapids I'll encounter.

Along my journey, people have floated into my life like leaves on a mountain stream. Some of them have floated away, either because of turbulence or a fork in the river. Some have floated back for a while. Some are still beside me. People have guided me through rapids by sharing what they've learned about themselves and the world. They taught me that mistakes aren't murderers; they're generally just misunderstandings, misperceptions, or miscommunications. Handled with care, mistakes can even become stones in foundations of solid, lasting relationships.

Thanks to those people, I've managed to make a few cherished friends. I'm starting to understand the value of family. I'm learning how to be a valued employee. I'm starting to experience the validation and enrichment of healthy relationships. My own relationships give me love, laughter, encouragement, and a safe haven from life's sometimes overwhelming chaos.

I'm starting to feel emotions I haven't yet experienced in my remembered life. Maybe I'm starting to know enough to be able to relate to what's happening around me. Maybe I'm starting to glimpse how full my past life might have been, and what people meant years ago when they said, "Your loss must be awful for you."

I'm now riding a relatively calm part of my river. For the most part, I'm happy with my life. It's simple. It's manageable for a nine-year-old. Even so, I know change is as inevitable as it is unpredictable. Change is also challenging. I hope I've learned enough to make the changes I'll face exciting, and fun.

A memorable life, however, like a raft trip, takes more than hope. None of us chooses our life's river. Each of us, however, chooses how we approach and navigate it. It doesn't take much to be mediocre. Just watching the river of life can be fascinating and wonderful if we choose to find a calm backwater and float lazily. However, to more fully experience the miracles of life and feel its exhilaration, we need to ride life's whitewaters.

We can ride those waters without a raft, but we won't get very far, and our trip will be rocky and treacherous. A well-designed craft, constructed with care, using the best materials—formal education and work—and modified with experiences picked up along the way, is our best bet for survival. A sturdy rudder—a goal—keeps us from going in circles. By staying on course, we can realize at least some of our dreams before our river freezes over and our journey ends. Our paddles—confidence, faith, common sense, and curiosity—keep us going, no matter what happens. Our life jackets—our friends—keep us afloat, especially when we're not sure we want to continue.

Our memories could be the one indispensable element of our journey. They're so integral to our lives that we can't imagine life without them. They make learning possible and help us develop resilience. They shape our dreams, our perspectives, our thoughts, our emotions, and our reactions.

Our memories make us real to each other. They help us decide whether we want to share part of our future with new acquaintances. They teach us how to relate to each other. They're the glue that keeps our relationships alive.

Memories remind us of where we've been, what we've done, what we've learned, and how we've felt. They help us decide our destination, chart our course, and navigate our lives' rivers. They're living color illustrations of who we are and what we value.

So, the next time some wise philosopher tells you that the only moment you have is now and advises you to forget your past, take a deep breath. Appreciate your memories. They're the brush strokes that add dimension to your life and color to your days. Recognize all of them—from the terrifying to the exhilarating—for the priceless miracles they are. After all, they could just disappear....

# Epilogue

*by Lorre Propst McKeone*

For the families and friends of those
with epilepsy

Epilepsy is a mystery for most people, and it certainly has been for our family. Because of our ignorance we did not have the first idea how the seizures should be treated or what the long-term impact of this brain disorder could be. Since my sister was an adult and living in another state, we didn't fully appreciate what a devastating impact this condition was having. Even now we are learning from her story in this book what we did not understand as she was living through it.

When my sister first started having seizures, we spent the first year consulting doctors who were unable to discover either the cause or a remedy for the seizures. This was the same year my mother was battling ovarian cancer. Our family was confronted with two difficult and unknown enemies. My mother lost her battle after thirteen months, and, as the family gathered for the funeral, my dad told Beki he wanted to send her to the Mayo Clinic to find out how to treat her seizures. A week later she called to tell us that even the famous Mayo Clinic seemed to have no answers for what was causing the seizures. Further, in the process of her extensive physical exams, they had detected a malignant lump in her breast. Reeling from the news of cancer in a second family member, the seizures took second place to the immediate concern of this new threat. What followed was a series of events that would have stunned the most resilient person. In the months and years that followed, my strong and independent sister endured a series of setbacks that would have shaken the most confident of people.

Our primary contact with Beki during this time was by telephone, and, for a while, it seemed that every phone call brought news of another crisis. She was treated successfully for the cancer but incurred medical bills that created financial difficulties. She had a college degree and had been successfully employed in professional positions but was unexpectedly terminated from her job over a dispute with her boss. Her husband announced that he wanted to experience the single life again before he was fifty and divorced her, leaving behind attorney bills and debts for her to repay. Her confidence crumbled, and she became disillusioned about her future. She continued to be employed, but it was largely in unsatisfactory, entry-level, low-paying positions. She was always looking for something else and was continually changing jobs. She became increasingly anxious and so volatile that we never knew what to expect when she called.

The one constant was the continuing seizures. She went to nearly every kind of doctor, therapist, or natural healer and tried a number of different antiseizure drugs, but nothing seemed to work. Because her behavior had become so unstable, we assumed she was having psychological difficulties. Our dad even consulted with a psychologist about how to help her. The advice we received was unproductive because it did not address the core issues of her seizures. Everything came to a head when she was found on a viaduct in a snowstorm, unconscious and with a high blood alcohol level. She nearly died from hypothermia, and the doctors told us they suspected she was an alcoholic. This led to a series of other interventions that, again, did not deal with the main problem she was facing.

What we didn't understand then, and have only begun to realize, is that the seizures may have been fundamental to nearly all of her other problems. Extreme mood swings appear to be a common characteristic of many people who suffer from epilepsy. The Epilepsy Foundation website shares this information about behavior during seizures:

> Seizure activity in the brain may affect speech, consciousness, and movement to such an extent that a person cannot respond or interact normally during the seizure or immediately afterward. Seizure symptoms may in rare cases include running, spitting, shouting, screaming, flailing movements, or abusive language. Remember that these actions are involuntary, not under conscious control. Confusion and disorientation may last for some time after a seizure ends, but will gradually improve.

In addition, a common side effect of many of the drugs used to treat seizures is erratic behavior and emotional instability. Since it is common for epileptics not to remember what happens during a seizure, those experiencing partial seizures may not even realize that their behavior has been erratic.

As Beki endured all of these difficult experiences, we assumed that her emotional outbursts and unpredictable behavior were a result of the troubles she was living through. Now we know that the seizures may have been largely responsible for the behaviors she exhibited and wonder if they were also a major contributor to her difficulties in her marriage and on the job.

It breaks my heart that we didn't realize what was happening at the time so that we could have been stronger advocates for her with medical professionals. Had we understood epilepsy better, perhaps we could have helped her find a remedy before she lost all her memories.

More than three million Americans live with epilepsy. Each year, two hundred thousand Americans will have a seizure for the first time. While epilepsy is one of the most common nervous system disorders, few understand it. If you or a friend or family member is suffering from seizures, I urge you to become better informed and to help in the efforts to find a cure. One of the best sources for information is the Epilepsy Foundation (http://www. epilepsyfoundation.org). From our experience it is clear that even many in the medical profession are not well versed in the intricacies of this disease. If you are not getting answers from the doctors that you consult, I urge you to ask your family doctor or a neurologist to refer you to an epileptologist (a doctor who specializes in epilepsy). I would also urge those in the medical profession to be more proactive in involving the extended family in fully understanding this condition so they can help.

I am grateful for the doctor who finally correctly diagnosed and treated my sister. While it appears that her seizures erased all her past memories, they did not damage her ability to learn and retain new knowledge. She has always been intelligent and intensely driven to excel. Her persistent refusal to give up in the face of incredible challenges has been an inspiration to all of us who did not have the first idea of how to help her. As she gradually learns how to navigate the world she woke up into, she is regaining her composure and confidence. Her behavior is no longer erratic, and I am increasingly seeing the fun and dynamic person I knew as my big sister when we were growing up. I have had to come to grips with the fact that all my past memories and experiences are largely irrelevant to my current relationship with Beki. But now that the seizures have been tamed, my sister is returning, and I look forward to making new memories together in the years to come.

# Appendix

## *What is Epilepsy?*

Epilepsy is one of the most common disorders of the nervous system. It affects people of all ages, races, and ethnic backgrounds. It can develop at any time of life.

Epilepsy is not a mental illness. It is not contagious. It is a disorder of the brain caused by temporary disturbances in the electrical activity of the brain's nerve cells. The brain is the control center for the body. Normal electrical signals between cells make the brain and body work correctly. The cells work like little switches, turning electrical charges on and off automatically.

A seizure is a kind of electrical power surge that happens when a group of nerve cells in the brain fire electrical impulses at a rate of up to four times higher than normal. This "brain storm" can spread to affect neighboring parts of the brain or, in some cases, the entire brain. Because certain parts of our brains are associated with specific functions, the symptoms produced by a seizure will depend on the area of the brain that is affected and how the abnormal electrical signals spread within the brain.

Just as many things can cause a headache, a seizure can be a symptom of many different types of brain irregularities. Partial seizures are the most common type of seizure experienced by people with epilepsy. They can affect not only movement, but also senses (including complex visual or auditory hallucinations) as well as emotions. In partial seizures, the electrical disturbance is limited to a specific area of the brain. If the brain storm causing the partial seizure spreads throughout the brain, it can cause a generalized (grand mal) seizure that causes the body to go into convulsions.

Some people have just one type of seizure. Others have more than one type. Although they look different, all seizures are caused by the same thing: a sudden change in the way the cells of the brain send electrical signals to each other.

Epilepsy can block out someone's usual awareness of his or her surroundings. It may change the way the world looks. It may make his or her body move automatically; it may cause a convulsion. Seizures usually last a short time, a matter of seconds or minutes, and end naturally as brain cell activity returns to normal. When the tempest ends, the person who had the seizure won't remember anything that happened during that seizure.

Some people may only have a single seizure during their lives. One seizure doesn't mean that a person has epilepsy. In fact, the term 'epilepsy' refers to a number of different kinds of recurring seizures that happen for a number of different reasons. With the exception of very young children and the elderly, the causes of most seizures are usually not identifiable.

(Sources: The Epilepsy Foundation, Novartis Pharmaceutical Corporation, MedicineNet.com.)

## Memory and Epilepsy

It's hard to find a definitive scientific explanation of memory. There are various theories, but the one that most closely fits my situation is described by Roberta Conlan in *The Incredible Voyage*. Her contention is that there are two major systems: "'knowing how' (implicit), or knowledge of motor skills, and 'knowing that' (declarative), knowledge of facts and events...." She explains:

> People who have suffered brain damage through accident or illness often retain some kinds of memory while losing others. Some may lose part of their long-term memory (the stable memory that lasts for days, weeks, and even a lifetime). Short-term (working) memory lasts only minutes and may be the loss others suffer.

Most people with epilepsy suffer some kind of memory loss. It makes sense that the excessive electrical activity in the brain during a seizure might damage the cells where memory is stored or the neurons that conduct electrical impulses to those cells. However, after years of research, there is only one thing I'm sure of: our understanding of the human brain is still extremely primitive.

Printed in the United States
124878LV00002B/97-102/A